Conte

C000101398

Chapter One: The Day Before Happys - Aiden's Story

You may think that suicide is a selfish escape. If so, the chances are you've never felt quite as helpless as I have for the last 363 days, twelve hours and forty-two minutes.

You may also be thinking that I'm simply being a hormonal, overdramatic 17-year-old boy who couldn't possibly know what hardship is.

Before you judge me or make your assumptions, try walking a mile in my shoes. I don't know who originally wrote that quote. I saw it posted the other day on Facebook by my mum's friend, Karen. I doubt they were her words though. She's not exactly the philosophical type. In fact, just thirty minutes later she posted her top ten reasons as to why her ex-husband was an absolute dickhead.

Anyhoo... I've been having a recurring dream almost every night for a couple of months now. In this dream, I'm stood on the edge of the roof upon a tall block of flats. I look towards the ten floors beneath me and feel at ease with the prospect of all the pain being over in one swift leap.

I take comfort in knowing I'll be relieving my friends and family of the burdens that come with dealing with someone as depressed as myself.

Sure, there'll be tears for the first few weeks, and a glass raised on Christmas and birthdays. Other than that, they'll continue on with their lives.

As a gust of wind edges me forward even closer to my impending death, I take it as a sign that this decision is for the best. Even the universe is encouraging me to leap and so... I do. I choose to say goodbye to all the hurt and pain.

It's only a mere second before impacting the ground that out of all the faces that could have popped into my mind's eye, it's that of Uncle Dave and in that moment, I regret it all.

Why my dad's brother of all people brought me peace, I have no idea. The man is the idiot of the family.

He has a terrible habit of saying the worst things at the most inappropriate times. Eventually, the family enforced a football penalty system upon him. Should Uncle Dave begin to go beyond the line of appropriateness, we'll announce, "*Yellow card*," - meaning he has been warned. Should he do or say something more extreme, he'll be presented with a stern, "*Red card*." When this happens, which is a lot, he is to either stop talking immediately, or vacate the area.

Idiot or otherwise, seeing his face was enough to ensure that I would wake up with a sense of relief that I was actually alive and safe. This feeling of solace would usually last approximately two minutes.

I mentioned this dream during one of our regular family counselling sessions a week ago. I wish I hadn't when I felt an instant change in the atmosphere.

The last time I saw my mum, dad and sister's faces all drop so dramatically was when Uncle Dave accidently texted nudes to the family WhatsApp group chat of ours - instead of sending them to Femi, who was his girlfriend at the time.

Their visible pain upon discovering just how low I had become was a hard pill to swallow. This was the very reason I'd never spoken up about my dark thoughts sooner. Why would I want to cause my family more hurt than they were already feeling? Yet that is precisely what I had done - like an absolute, selfish idiot.

I tried to play it down and make out I'd only had this dream once, maybe twice before. Of course, the counsellor knew I was lying. You know, they're actually trained to spot lies with the slightest movement of a person's finger, or their eyes looking in a particular direction. This is precisely why I could never be in a relationship with one.

After failing miserably to lie my way through the long, gruelling session where I had made my revelation, the counsellor requested us all to leave the room - everyone except my mum - and it didn't take a genius to work out what they were 'discreetly' discussing.

The moment I fell asleep that evening, my mum spent the next few hours hiding every knife, fork and anything else even remotely sharp in the house, along with any medication that was previously accessible. She even went as far as to put rubber shields over any piece of furniture with a pointy edge - apparently confusing my being suicidal with me being a toddler.

I'd like to stress that I didn't actually want to kill myself. At least, I didn't think I did. I believe I was merely, but deeply fed up with day to day life. It seemed like I couldn't please one person without pissing off another, there was always one drama, or form of chaos taking place in school or online and I couldn't even switch the television on without being reminded that things were awful everywhere. For instance, there's actually a man from my own city on the run after having killed his wife. Apparently, these things don't just happen in movies - but practically on my own doorstep and naturally, everyone local was talking about it. There was literally no escaping the ever expanding cloud of negativity.

As a consequence of everyone now thinking I wanted to end it all, it was decided that I would attend the next counselling session alone. I had no say in this decision. I was reluctant to go on my own, but if it meant my mum regaining some sanity by returning the liquorice laces to the cupboard - indeed concerned that I may attempt to strangle myself with them - then it was worth the hour of awkward silence.

In reality, the solo session was even more unpleasant than I could have ever imagined.

With the worst night of my life just two days away from its one-year anniversary, and not having my annoying sister taking up a large chunk of session time - due to loving the sound of her own voice - I felt like I was truly in the spotlight and I found myself even more anxious as a result.

I wasn't ready to talk about that night, almost one year back. Not to my family, not to friends and certainly not to someone I saw for one hour each week. So, I simply sat in silence looking around the room, studying it intently.

It was the first time I'd noticed just how cliché this room was. The gentle humming of the fish tank, the flowers, books, tidy desk and the duck egg blue paint were supposed to soothe me, according to research, no doubt.

This is the first reason why I hate this world. Whether it be through society's expectations, science or whatever other potential facet - we're constantly being told how we should be thinking, feeling and living our lives. We're supposed to happily live in the box we've been placed in and should we dare to try and break the seal, so as to venture out of it, we're looked at and relabelled as weirdo's. I'm told what sauce I should be having with certain meats; I'm supposed to hold a conversation about football because I'm male. As a kid, I was encouraged to question my surroundings by teachers and other authoritative figures, but only up until a certain age - at which point I'm supposed to accept what I'm told by society, or be branded a conspiracy nut. I also played with toys as a child because it's a natural instinct to do so... but again, at a certain age we're supposed to cut that shit out too.

The more we're told how to think, the less we actually think for ourselves, until eventually, we forget how to.

Like I said, I've no doubt that research has concluded numerous times that the duck egg blue paint was supposed to soothe me - and for that reason, it pissed me right off.

And breathe.

I'd almost managed to avoid answering any difficult questions for the entire session when the counsellor knocked me sideways with a statement I hadn't expected.

"Aiden... how would you feel if I told you that what happened that night... it wasn't your fault?" she asked softly.

I couldn't quite process the thoughts that came flooding through my mind. I think mostly, I felt anger that she would have the audacity to make such a statement.

"You're wrong," I snapped. "If it weren't for me and my actions that night then maybe..."

I couldn't finish the sentence. Instead, I wept uncontrollably - perhaps more than I had ever done before.

When the tears eventually stopped pouring, I croaked the words, "I'm sorry."

"You have no reason to apologise."

I wiped the tears from my face and took it upon myself to officially end the session by standing up to put on my coat. As I was doing so, the counsellor began to talk to me in a slightly more informal off-the-clock tone. "Try to enjoy your weekend at Happys," she said with a comforting smile. "Get involved in the activities. Talk to a girl. It could be fun."

I nodded, but of course I knew it wouldn't be a fun weekend away. A Happys caravan holiday is not somewhere families go for fun, but more to continue on tradition. Before the days of Internet, gaming and pizza delivered straight to your door, my grandparents would take my mum and dad on a Happys holiday every year, as I can only assume, there was nothing better to do at home. My parents continued this tradition with my sister and I. One day, I'll likely force my kids to go too.

Just as I was about to leave the room, the counsellor called out with a sense of urgency. "Aiden, one last thing before you go. I remember a few months back, your mother spoke so proudly about you being quite the song writer and I thought-"

"I don't really do music anymore," I interrupted.

"I know. But maybe you should. You don't want to talk openly about what happened that night and I completely understand that. Instead, please consider writing about how you feel... in the form of a song perhaps? Nobody has to see, read or hear what you've written. It can be for you and you alone."

"Maybe," I shrugged. I knew she'd assume that her words were going in one ear and straight out of the other, but I actually meant it. It wasn't a terrible idea. In fact, I made a pact with myself right then, that by the end of the weekend I would have a song completed. God knows I needed the distraction.

Regardless as to whether it was my well-overdue cry, or the fact I was given an idea I could finally get on board with, I walked out of this counselling session feeling somewhat optimistic. As was always the case, this feeling didn't last long.

Waiting for me at the corner of the building was Uncle Dave. I thought I had no tears left to cry but apparently this wasn't the case. I had to fight back those flood gates opening again as I marched right past him.

He did what can only be described as a 'panto skip' to keep up with me.

"Where's mum?" I screamed whilst speeding up.

"You know where she is," he said, surprisingly breathless, considering we had literally only just started this passive-aggressive workout.

"I guess I just thought that she wouldn't actually go. Not tonight. Not this weekend."

"Like all of us, your mother needs to try and live her life normally," he said, even more out of breath.

"But now? Really?"

"Look… can we stop for a moment?" he pleaded.

I stopped with a genuine fear that he could actually have a heart-attack.

I looked at Uncle Dave shamefully, reminding him, "You were saying just the other week that you could easily run a marathon. I remember it well. You'd just bitten into your seventh sausage."

"Well, I haven't warmed up."

As another tear raced down my cheek, Uncle Dave comfortingly put his hands on my shoulders. His sleeveless t-shirt revealed what are probably the most fascinating arms I've ever seen. Covered in scars, he'd often tell random girls he fancied that he'd obtained these injuries as a result of the line of work he was in. Naturally, they would assume that my Uncle was some kind of fighter - perhaps even a spy. Of course, he'd never correct them that actually, he worked in a cafe and was incapable of using an oven or panini machine without burning himself. If you ever heard him shouting profanities from the kitchen, you knew dinner was about to be served. His right arm also had a tattoo of the British singer, Cliff Richard - who was surrounded by other dark unidentifiable figures. Random? Yes. I'll explain all in good time.

Uncle Dave looked stuck on what to say to me at first, before awkwardly asking, "Do you still want to kill yourself?"

Chances are, he would have been asked to discreetly question me on my current mental state, but Uncle Dave doesn't do discreet.

"No, I'm fine."

"That's great news," he said, appearing to be completely convinced by the blatant lie. "I have perfected the recipe for my famous homemade burgers - not to mention the homemade crispy chips on the side. I'm cooking for you all tonight and if you were dead... well, you'd totally be missing out."

These words were actually coming out of his mouth.

"And I have even more good news," he continued. "I'll be joining you at Happys over the weekend. You've got yourself a wing-man. Mothers, lock up your legally of age and fully consenting daughters - Aiden and Uncle Dave are on our way. Of course, I won't personally be getting involved with any young girls. I'll just be watching."

Whilst becoming flustered, he continued, "Not watching anything dodgy. Just watching on as you chat to-"

"You know what, I'm giving you a yellow card before this conversation gets even weirder."

"That's fair."

Uncle Dave was clearly just coming along for the weekend to help ensure I didn't do anything stupid. The irony being, if anything was going to push me to actually take my own life, it'd be not being able to escape this buffoon for the next couple of days.

The moment we got home, I stormed to my bedroom. I just wanted to be on my own.

My room was pretty standard for someone of my age. I had my bed, an old couch and a couple of games consoles - not that you could see them underneath the mountain of dirty clothes flung on top.

Surrounded by a dozen Foo Fighters posters, my acoustic guitar proudly hung centrally, on the wall. For the first time in around six months, I wrapped my fingers around it, lifting it from the wall mount.

The familiar grasp invoked old memories that came flooding back.

These memories were a reminder that I never used to be this angry at the world. I used to look forward to things. I was happy. I was in a band. I chose to be around people and I was at my happiest in the company of my band mates. We'd literally belly-laugh at every single practice. I think the last time we were all together was the last time I laughed out loud authentically.

I hadn't thought about these people since moving schools. Although now nothing more than distant memories, it was interesting to discover that these thoughts could still make me smile.

Perhaps this was a turning point.

This would be my first attempt at writing a song in a fair while. I'd written a few since the incident but found each song was getting more aggressive than the last. By the fourth song, I was starting to scare myself. My lyrics had become overwhelmingly confronting.

Ready to get my creative juices flowing again, I flopped onto my bed to get comfortable for the hours that lay ahead.

The moment I made contact with the sheets, I felt as if the ground below me was crumbling. It took me straight back to the sensation of falling from the building in my dreams. My heart raced and I began to struggle to breathe. Although it would have likely only been a few seconds, it felt like minutes had passed until the reality had kicked in.

My bed had been replaced by empty boxes, with sheets thrown over them to trick me. Sorry, to prank me - and I had no doubt that my sister, Tracey, was the culprit. For someone just two years younger than me, it was startling just how different we were.

To no surprise, she was suddenly stood above me, camcorder in hand.

"To the haters that thought my brother wouldn't be stupid enough to fall for this prank, you were wrong," she enthusiastically said to the camera. "To all those in Team Tracey that knew I'd pull it off... love to you."

A switch flicked in my head. All pleasant thoughts I previously had of better days were replaced with a blind rage. I'd had enough of my ignorant family and wanted to smash my sisters' bloody camera beyond repair.

Tracey knew it.

"I'm sorry. It was just a joke," she pleaded.

I leapt up and marched towards her, which left my sister squirming with fear.

She held the camera behind her back to protect it, whilst reaching towards me with the other hand to protect herself.

Later, that look of fear would haunt me. But in that very moment, I had things that I felt my sister needed to hear. "I'm done playing your games," I screamed.

"I know... I know. I'm sorry," she said softly. This was in contrast to her usual argumentative nature. Perhaps she had truly realised that a line had been crossed.

"Play your stupid games with your stupid friends all you like, just keep me out of it."

"I can't upload a video for the next three days so I wanted to make this particular one a gooden."

"You can't upload for three whole days? How awful," I said sarcastically. "Who cares? You have two subscribers and one of them is me. I can therefore confirm that at least half of your following does not give a shit about you!"

Maybe Tracey had good reason to squirm before. These weren't the kind of words that usually came out of my mouth. Who had I become?

I could see the hurt in her eyes. It echoed the look of disappointment coming from my dad, who was stood at my bedroom door. I don't know how long he had been there but it was definitely long enough to have witnessed one of my lowest moments.

As Tracey left the room in tears. I slumped, with shame to the floor.

"I didn't mean that."

I could suddenly hear Uncle Dave screaming profanities from the kitchen. I was relieved by the thought of being called down for dinner any moment - releasing me from this mortifying situation.

"I know," my dad said softly whilst sitting beside me. "But you have to realise that your actions have consequences."

"Trust me, I know that more than anybody."

"Then you should know more than anybody that you should think before you speak. I don't want to hear you talk to your sister like that again."

"I won't," I croaked, riddled with guilt.

"When life gives you lemons, you shouldn't then throw those lemons at other people like a little dickhead," he teased before changing the subject. "Aiden, I've been meaning to say something for a while. I'm hoping this could be something that you want to hear. It may not be. I... I forgive Danny Palmer. Maybe it's time for you to forgive him too? If you like, we can arrange a visi-"

"No. No, thank you," I croaked.

"I understand," Dad said softly before vacating the room.

Some would say that I got off lightly with my dad, considering the shocking way I'd spoken to my sister. After all, he didn't even raise his voice. Actually, I'd have preferred the angry side of him as opposed to disappointed. That look had always killed me.

It was a matter of seconds before Uncle Dave then walked in with dinner plates in hand. He also had that all too familiar look of disappointment, directed straight towards me. "I heard all of that commotion from downstairs. Not cool" he said sternly.

"I know, I'm sorry. I'll apologise to Tracey soon."

I couldn't help but notice the lack of food on the plates that he was carrying. Both contained nothing more than a half-eaten burger.

Uncle Dave declared, "I've got your dinner here but as a punishment for your shocking behaviour, I took a few bites from your burger and ate all your chips."

"You ate those chips long before Tracey and I argued, didn't you?"

He gave me the classic 'smart ass' look whilst handing me what little food remained, before making a swift exit.

I could hear the distinct sound of my mum's footsteps heading up the stairs. She was back much sooner than expected. I hoped this was a sign that her night had also gone badly. This may sound harsh, but I was still rather bitter about her choice to go out tonight.

"I hope you're hungry," I heard Uncle Dave say to her.

"Starving."

"Good, there's a burger sitting in the microwave, but... I'm afraid I burnt the chips and had to bung them in the bin."

"You ate them whilst dishing up, didn't you?"

"I did, yes," he responded shamefully.

I heard a frustrated sigh from my mother before her footsteps continued in my direction.

I prepared myself for the next round of 'let's tell Aiden how awful he is.' What I didn't expect was her appearance. Mum was covered in what looked like the icing from a cake - with splashes from head to toe. In her hand was an opened bottle of wine.

"I don't want to know what happened," she said to me whilst looking at the collapsed boxes.

"Good, because I really don't want to talk about it."

"How was today's session?"

"I don't want to talk about that either if you don't mind. What happened to you?"

Mum gave out a defeated laugh. "You wouldn't believe me if I told you," she said before guzzling a large mouthful of wine straight from the bottle. "But you'll likely be pleased to know that my night went very badly."

"What? No." I said unconvincingly.

She took another swig from the bottle.

"You don't want a glass for that?" I asked.

"No, I'm good. It goes down the same hole either way."

The moment my mum left the room, I sprinted to the door to close it before anyone else decided to pay me a visit. I'd desperately wanted an evening to myself but my bedroom had turned into Piccadilly bloody Circus.

Knowing her night was a disaster was comforting. It was certainly enough to push me to get back on track with the writing. Once again, I picked up the guitar. I may not have been in the right frame of mind to write an entire song, but I figured even a few lines would be better than none.

As I collapsed onto the couch, that also broke beneath me. Yep, more boxes. Boxes stacked up in the shape of the furniture with a large throw blanket over it. At this point I wasn't even mad. I no longer possessed the energy required to be mad. I just lay there, numb – reflecting on what a weird evening it had been.

Little did I know at the time, the next couple of days were going to get a hell of a lot weirder.

Chapter Two: We're all going on a shoddy holiday - Aiden's Story

It's been a long time since I stepped foot inside of a car. My entire body just freezes up every time I try.

Credit where credit is due - when I expressed that my preferred method of transport to Happys was the train, despite it being the least convenient way to travel there, the whole family were supportive of the decision. I was truly grateful for that.

Considering they made that effort for me without an ounce of hesitation, I wanted to do something for them. I made the conscious effort to start the weekend on a good note.

Before we set off, I made everyone breakfast in the morning for the first time since... actually, it was the very first time. Not only that, I chose to wear an item of clothing that I knew would bring Mum joy. It was something that I usually detested wearing because of the verbal abuse it often attracted.

Now, a side-effect of my depression is not caring as much what others think of me. Used correctly, it's almost like a superpower. On this particular day, I wore my white t-shirt with the words 'Mummy's Little Princess' written on it and I genuinely didn't care who might see it.

How did this monstrosity end up in my possession, you may be wondering? A few years back, during a school trip to our local swimming pool, I was unfortunately chosen to clean up after the class at the end of our session. Avoiding eye-contact with our teacher as he chose his victim had not helped me this time.

After five minutes of collecting inflatable pool floats, which were mostly used as weapons for us students to beat the crap out of each other with, I was last into the changing room. This meant I was first choice to be picked for an elaborate prank.

The clothes I had bought with me had been replaced with a skimpy pair of shorts and the unflattering top. With nothing else that fit me in lost property, I was forced to spend the rest of the school day declaring I was, in fact, Mummy's Little Princess.

Could my fellow classmates have leant me a jumper or coat? Of course. Did they? Absolutely not.

Once I made it home that evening - surprisingly not beaten and bruised - Mum took one look at the t-shirt and laughed uncontrollably.

During the years that would follow, she'd plead with me to wear it - particularly on each Mother's Day. In her words, I had to do as I was told on that day as it was 'her' day.

To Mum's joy, I'd wear it at home from time to time. I just couldn't bare wearing it in public.

After the longest time of constantly being jeered at, that I was a Princess whilst walking through the school corridors, it started to become less frequent in more recent months. I wasn't going to risk refuelling that fire.

The morning of our trip to Happys, not only was I wearing the t-shirt outside of the house, I didn't even feel the slightest bit self-conscious.

In comparison to once caring so deeply what everyone thought of me consuming my mind, this newly acquired indifference felt like an actual superpower. I felt free.

As I'd hoped, Mum appeared to appreciate the gesture. Passing her on the train, I noticed her glance in my direction before grinning ear to ear. This must have been the twelfth time I'd seen her do so that morning. It wasn't the forced smile I'd become so accustomed to.

Despite being crammed into the trains' hot and stuffy carriage, the entire family looked to be in fairly high spirits.

Mum was sat beside my sister, who was typically scrolling through her phone. Tracey clearly saw something on the screen that excited her, as she gave out a little squeal. I can only assume she had just gotten her third subscriber - someone else in the family, most likely.

Dad was selflessly stood up, knowing others would no doubt appreciate a seat more than himself.

Then there was Uncle Dave, who was sat beside me. I knew this meant conversations would be limited to either the ever increasing price of a Freddo chocolate bar, or unwanted details of the erotic romance novel he was writing. He once described it as a feminist remake of '50 Shades of Grey', in which the roles were reversed. The work in progress is titled, 'Right, now it's my turn!' An entire family counselling session was once dedicated entirely to the mortifying time Uncle Dave read us his first chapter out loud.

Of course, I'd grin and bear whatever he had to say on this occasion. It was a sacrifice I was willing to make; given I had deprived everyone of the opportunity of a simple drive directly to our caravan door.

The sudden motion of our train departing from the platform caused each passenger to jerk forwards. This was enough to startle the toddler sat on his mother's lap in the seat directly in front of me.

The child, who can't have been more than 2-years-old, began to scream at the top of his lungs.

That all-too-familiar anger within me, slowly started to increase and threatened to boil over. I tried desperately to fight against it.

I wanted to keep this well-overdue positive energy high for the sake of the family, but with every scream coming from that child, I began to lose the battle little by little.

I was not actually angry for the reason you may think.

I looked around towards the rest of the passengers and most were making no attempt to hide their frustration caused by the distressed child.

Some shook their heads whilst others stared at the young boy with eyes piercing through him, powerful enough to kill. Other's went as far as tutting out loud - which is our passive, British way of communicating that, "*I am very pissed off.*"

Well, I was pissed off at the attitudes of these supposed adults, which leads me to the second reason why I hate this world.

At most, we'd have to put up with this crying for an hour. As far as we knew, this could have been typical behaviour for the child for so many different reasons, unbeknownst to any of us. The mother could be severely sleep-deprived as a result. Yet, these adults couldn't muster a shred of feigned apathy, or better yet, invoke any empathy for sixty-minutes? Most people lack the ability to look at the potentially bigger picture - like they're incapable of looking beyond what they see in any given moment.

But... I don't know. Maybe I was on par for not considering there could be a good reason as to why these passengers were stressed out by the child? Who knows.

Instead of stewing on these thoughts, I decided instead to take action. I locked eyes with the toddler and as if a switch had been flicked, his tears were suddenly replaced with the most adorable laugh.

For reasons that alluded me, kids had always been drawn to me.

The toddler hid his face into his mother's chest, giving me the occasional glance before quickly hiding again. I knew this meant game on. We had officially embarked upon a classic round of Peekaboo.

"Where is he? Where's the boy gone?" I asked in a childish, exaggerated manner.

Uncle Dave looked confused. "Dude, what's wrong with you," he said genuinely bewildered. "He's right there."

Trust me, he really was not joking.

"Yes... thank you," I replied.

My uncle laughed at what he was assuming to be my own stupidity before declaring, "Can you believe that a cheese sandwich on this train costs six pounds?"

"No, I can't believe it," I said humouring him, knowing exactly what was coming next.

"I dread to think how much they would charge for a Freddo."

"Tell me about it.'" I said with forced enthusiasm. In hindsight, it wasn't the best choice of words. He did just that for the remainder of the train journey. Still, I'd rather the Freddo talk over the gut-wrenching details of his novel.

The walk from the train station to Happys couldn't have taken more than thirty minutes, but by the time we'd reached the destination with our weighty bags in hand, we had built up quite the sweat and were all physically exhausted. Dropping those bags at the reception area felt like throwing the ring into Mordor. A great weight had been lifted.

Amazingly, spirits were still fairly high amongst everyone. I had been expecting little digs and passive-aggressive comments, but thankfully they never came.

I'm almost certain I would have received a justified berating from my mother in particular, if it weren't for the fact that we had made it just in time for the traditional Happys welcome event.

By the way, don't be fooled into thinking the word 'event' automatically translates to mean anything that will be remotely enjoyable. Technically, a funeral could be described as an 'event'.

This particular weekly presentation was an opportunity for guests to discover what activities were upcoming on-site, whilst hearing about the local shops and arcades outside of the Happys bubble. It was the same, repetitive information each time, but with the talk came a free glass of Sangria for each adult, which is presumably why Mum was always adamant we attend.

To say she had always enjoyed an alcoholic beverage would be an understatement. Even so, in recent months I feared Mum had become dependent on the stuff. With this in mind, I was apprehensive as to how the next thirty minutes or so might play out. I preferred to think she'd take the free beverage and stop there - stepping up as a responsible mother at a time we needed her the most - with a clear and level head on her shoulders. However, it was much more likely that the Sangria would be just the start of many more drinks to come throughout the day.

It was time to find out.

Chapter Three: Welcome to Happys - Aiden's Story

The half-hour of welcome event hell always took place within the large entertainment hall. This venue consisted of a stage and lighting rig - of which, half of the lights were broken. There was also a bar - unsurprisingly busy, despite it being 11am - and filling up the remainder of the space, there were about one hundred tables filled mostly with middle-aged people looking even more depressed than I was.

Strangely, in previous years, the hall had always seemed so bright and full of life, but as I sat here now, I felt like I was sat in a rescue centre and we were located slap bang in the middle of it.

Beside me at our table was Tracey, who was intensely looking through her phone - I know, big surprise. Dad and Uncle Dave were busy taking our bags to the caravan before attempting to secure us sun loungers in a decent spot. As for mum - disappointingly but unsurprisingly - she was at the bar and I could see a large glass of wine being poured for her.

This all but confirmed that Tracey and I would need to make it through the next two days without her support.

I needed a distraction.

Knowing I'd get no interaction from my sister whilst her mobile had battery life and with no sign of the presentation starting any time soon, I waved to grab the attention of a waitress handing out the sangria.

"What's up?" she asked.

"Do you happen to have a pen and paper I can use?"

She rifled through her large hip bag before pulling out a box of crayons and a small piece of paper filled with puzzles designed for small children. "You're welcome to use the blank side of this?"

"That'll be great, thank you."

I gracefully took the items with the intention of killing some time, noting down my feelings in the form of song lyrics, as requested by the family Counsellor. It was a productive use of time in theory, but it didn't take me long to realise that the words just simply weren't going to come.

Back in the day, I'd have effortlessly thrown together half a dozen original songs in a few hours but now I couldn't even string together a single sentence.

Waiting and hoping for inspiration to strike, I decide to play a solo game of Happys Bingo.

There were certain guarantees of things you were going to see on a low-budget UK caravan holiday park such as Happys. For example, the dance floor area was packed with children skidding on their knees. It was an unwritten rule for kids not to wear their best trousers in the entertainment hall for this very reason.

These kids were, of course, unsupervised. Within the walls of Happys, the parents like to take a step back and let their hair down, whilst leaving it to the staff to stress over the potential damages to the surroundings and to the kids themselves.

Another tick on my metaphorical bingo card came in the form of some random, obese man stood at the bar, wearing nothing but a pair of Speedos. The fact that it was jacket weather was irrelevant. It could be chucking it down with rain and nobody would bat an eyelid at such a sight somewhere like here. However, attempt to chill at the bar wearing Speedos at any family venue outside of a seaside resort and the police will most definitely be escorting you to the station.

Once I was able to divert my eyes from the magnetic force of those Speedos, I caught another glimpse of Mum. I was heartbroken to see her so blatantly flirting with the young guy serving her. He must have been about twenty-five - basically half her age.

There was nothing he could be saying to make her genuinely laugh in such an animated manner and there was no way their hands should have touched for as long as they did, whilst her two glasses of wine were passed over.

I was furious.

It seems the moment my dad was gone; she'd be ready to pounce on any guy that threw a smile in her direction.

Once she returned to the table, I couldn't contain my feelings. "You and that barman looked like you were having fun," I yelled, fiercely.

"As a matter of fact, we were. Is that okay?" Mum responded with a much softer tone.

"Well, I hope you find genital herpes fun because that's what you'll get mixing with a guy like that."

Ah, crap.

I'd done it again. I had crossed another line.

It was a statement so bad that Tracey's eyes diverted away from her phone for a brief moment with a look that said, "*You've fucked up.*"

It mirrored Mum's expression.

Just as she was about to give me the inevitable bollocking, we were interrupted by the waitress. "Complimentary sangria, sir?" she asked me.

Mum jumped in with, "Actually, he's not quite old enough to drink yet."

"And even if I was, I wouldn't be drinking alcohol anyway."

I felt that it was important to make this statement. Mum disagreed. "She doesn't care, sweetie... but I will take mine and the one you offered him," she said whilst grabbing two glasses.

The waitress gave that classic 'I don't care' smile before returning to her duties.

Mum took a moment to gather her thoughts. I genuinely had no idea what level of wrath she was about to unleash upon me but I felt my self tensing, bracing myself for it.

"We're all dealing with things in our own way," she said surprisingly calm.

I can only assume that the fact she now had four alcoholic drinks lined up in front of her, helped lighten her mood.

Mum took a large sip of her first glass of wine before continuing, "Maybe coming here was a bad idea. Maybe it's just another constant reminder of that person. If so, give me the word and we'll pack up and leave with no questions asked. All I ask is whilst we are here, we try to make it work. Is that fair?"

I tried to respond verbally but the words wouldn't come out. The story of my life right now. I simply nodded instead.

Mum downed the remainder of the drink.

I'd considered ranting about how irresponsible her day drinking was. I desperately wanted to explain just how inappropriate and disrespectful I also found her flirting to be. Now was not the time though. Like Mum said, we were here and we had to try and make it work for... the.... okay... hold up.

Just a few tables across from us was the most gorgeous girl I had ever seen in my entire life. Seeing someone at this level of beauty had not made it onto my bingo game in all of my years coming to Happys because it had never happened.

She was petite. This was the first huge tick for my fragile, emasculated - due to my own lack of height - self. She was also athletic and looked to be similar in age to me, perhaps a year or two older. She was the classic cute girl next door type, which was right up my street. In fact, it was like every porn site I'd ever visited had accumulated the data from my search history and this beautiful specimen is what the algorithm spat out.

Dear God, I was starting to sound like my Uncle Dave. Apologies. Believe it or not, I do have a romantic side, but, well, this is not The Notebook and as you know, my creative juices had not exactly been flowing.

She was just... incredible.

I was intensely captivated by her hazel eyes and matching coloured hair, which flowed down to her jeans. It was when she flicked that hair back behind her that I just knew the stars had well and truly aligned. I suddenly clocked that she was wearing a Dave Grohl t-shirt. Yup, the lead singer of my favourite band was painted on the love of my life. I literally owned that very same top.

I can only assume it was a combination of all of these amazing qualities that left me staring at her in the same way that someone ten days into their diet might look at a takeaway flyer just posted through their letterbox.

It was at that very moment we locked eyes and... she looked terrified. I can't say I blamed her.

I literally could not stop staring. I could not stop smiling either. I was like a deer in headlights – captivated and in complete awe.

As I gazed towards her awkwardly, a devastating realisation hit me with the force of an entire stampede. Not only was I wearing my 'Mummy's Little Princess' t-shirt but, from her point of view, I was also colouring with crayons. If there was a starter pack designed for people never wanting to get laid, these items would most definitely be in it.

The tractor beam I was trapped within, was finally broken thanks to an elbow smacking into the back of my head. I say "thanks to" because I was authentically thankful to once again be in control of my actions, but I was also rather outraged. The smack felt intentional and frankly, it really hurt.

My suspicions of deliberate foul play grew stronger upon hearing the most insincere apology imaginable. "Sorry, maaaate," said this random guy, who looked to be in his late twenties and wearing a t-shirt with his very own face printed onto it.

Upon hearing this guy's voice, Tracey's mobile flew from her hands. She began to freak out in her excitement. It turns out that this random elbow greeter was, in fact, a God in her eyes.

"Was Lee Lauren just talking to you?" she squealed excitedly - almost hyperventilating.

"Who?"

"Internet Sensation... Lee Lauren... The titty guy!"

"The what guy?"

My sister intensely leaned in closer towards me. "Lee Lauren gets millions of views on every single video he uploads," she said. "The legend exploded after posting a video at some coffee place in London. He suffered with a stutter at the time and the more he struggled to ask for a cup of tea, the more it sounded like he was shouting 'titties'. Off the back of that video, thousands of other clips surfaced from all around the world - showing people running into their local coffee shop, shouting 'titties'."

A memory that had been buried alongside other seemingly insignificant details swiftly resurfaced. I explained, "Now that you mention it, I do remember ordering an iced coffee a while back and some guy behind me did indeed shout 'titties'. I just assumed he was mentally challenged."

I could see this 'titty guy' posing for pictures with a couple of female teens that had practically jumped on him. He was lapping up their attention.

I couldn't quite tell what he was saying to them but both girls suddenly looked quite disheartened before passing him over some of their money.

Surely he hadn't just asked them for this cash?

Also, something about him being here didn't quite add up. "If he's this big shot in the world of entertainment, what's he doing at Happys?" I asked curiously.

"I know, right," Tracey said. "He posted earlier saying he was going to be here all weekend filming an advert for them. This used to be his go-to family holiday destination growing up. In fact, he was literally here last year when his titty video blew up - making him famous within hours. Maybe he feels this place brings him luck. Maybe he doesn't want to forget his humble roots by helping the little people. I don't know. It's just weird that two weeks ago I'm watching him cameo in a hilarious Adam Sandler movie and now he's here, of all the places."

"Something else doesn't add up," I said.

"Go on."

"Adam Sandler made a hilarious movie?"

Tracey didn't seem amused by this joke. Dad would have loved it.

I watched in horror as this apparent celebrity approached the girl I was besotted with. He dominantly pinched her chin before pulling her face towards his for a long, passionate kiss. He maintained eye-contact with me the entire time. I believe the term to best describe this masculine parade is 'peacocking'.

This pretty much confirmed my previous suspicion that the hard whack to the back of my head was no accident. He clearly saw me gawping and took action. Fair enough, I guess.

"Who's the girl he's with?" I asked.

"That's Lee Lauren's fiancé, Alizia Cox. They've been together two months."

"Engaged for two months?"

"No, they met two months ago."

Blimey. Possibly the fastest proposal in history but again, looking at her, fair enough.

"And what's Alizia's story?" I attempted to ask in a non-desperate or stalker sounding way.

"She is a famous makeup artist. Well, she was. Alizia Cox can make herself look like a completely different person using just makeup - it's crazy impressive. She recently quit posting videos and came off her socials entirely to commit herself full time to Lee Lauren's busy schedule - which is so cute."

"And so unnecessary."

Tracey slid her phone towards me. On the screen was a variety of Lee's videos. I scrolled through them and just as my sister had said, the viewer numbers were insane - some reaching more than ten million per upload. The video simply titled 'Titties' had almost double that amount. The fact that the thumbnail image was actually a pair of giant breasts may have contributed to its popularity.

I clicked on what appeared to be the second most popular video. Titled, 'I'm on a Train - Toot Toot, Bitches'. The five seconds of footage was Lee stood in a packed London Underground carriage, shouting, "I'm on a Train - Toot Toot, Bitches."

Below that video was a link to his merch store, where you could purchase a t-shirt with the words "I'm on a Train - Toot Toot, Bitches" printed on it.

Upon further inspection, I had a sneaking suspicion that maybe the severe hardships presented to him throughout his life were greatly exaggerated - if not entirely fabricated. That may sound harsh given that I knew very little about Lee. However, alongside the struggles with his stutter, based on his video titles, he's also had battles with colour blindness, diabetes, a stalker, poltergeists and a murderous midget zombie that had been visiting him every morning at 3am.

Perhaps my opinion of this guy was clouded by the fact he was in a relationship with the most beautiful person I'd seen in my life, but I just didn't get it. I didn't understand how shouting 'Titties' and 'Toot Toot, Bitches' could bring someone fame, fortune and more importantly, a goddess by their side.

This is another reason why I hate this world. We look at famous people as...

Luckily for you, my internal rant was interrupted by music blaring out from the speakers. This meant that the welcome event had officially begun.

I recognised the song instantly as 'Let Me Entertain You' by Robbie Williams.

I cringed, already knowing what was coming next. The full house on my imaginative Bingo card came courtesy of the inevitable appearance of The Taylor Twins, a forty-something-year-old, larger than life, brother/sister duo - also known as the Happys entertainment team. They were... intense. I once saw Tommy and Tammy both high-five a waiter for receiving what they enthusiastically announced to be the perfect amount of ice cubes in their glass of water.

Mid way through the songs' instrumental intro, the twins skipped onto the stage whilst encouraging the audience to clap along to the track.

Of course, nobody clapped along. It was 11am after all.

I'm not sure that the pair of them fully understood the concept of a microphone because they screeched into them like they were trying to be heard by the people in the back of the hall.

In the first verse of the song are the lyrics, "Shake your arse, come over here, now scream!" At this point The Taylor Twins held out their microphones, encouraging the audience to scream.

Nobody screamed.

The song faded out after the first chorus. Thank God, as I was struggling to endure the extreme level of cringe.

After what seemed like awkwardly waiting for an applause that just didn't come, Tommy screamed into his microphone, "We're The Taylor Twins. You're awesome. Your holiday starts right now!"

The sister took over. "I'm Tammy," she screamed. "To my left is Tommy and new to the team over in the sound box is a newbie to this entertainment team. He's only been with us for a couple of weeks but we already consider him a close friend. Say 'Hello' to these wonderful people, Ben!"

"My name is Dan," said a spiritless voice from the speakers.

In recent years, the sound person had been the young daughter of the owner of Happys. When I say young, I mean it - so much so that I'm almost certain child exploitation laws had been broken having her work here. She'd always looked miserable doing her job. Her name was... Jenny Happy, if my memory serves me right. She got along really well with my sister. I can only assume Jenny escaped this place the moment she was old enough to do so. Even I was tempted to run away and I'd not even been here for half an hour.

The Twins smiled uncomfortably for a few moments due to the name mix-up. Tommy took charge in swiftly moving on. "It's not just Dan who is new to Happys," he said. "This summer we have opened the thrilling 'Dynamite Diving Board'. Measuring at twelve metres, it's a whopping two metres taller than what they use in the Olympics!"

Tommy continued, "We have also re-opened our main restaurant since the court deemed Happys are not responsible for the situation that the media dubbed 'The Diarrhoea Massacre'. The slight stench of excrement may still be lingering but our reputation now smells of roses. Also, we know you're all dying to hear what entertainment we have on offer over the next week. Well, every night from 6pm, we have your kids mini disco, bingo at 7 and your main event at 8."

Tommy high-fived his sister, passing over the figurative baton. "Tonight at 8pm is our favourite pirate themed 80's tribute band, Arrr-Ha," Tammy said. "Throughout the week we have magicians, drag acts, dancers and even a hypnotist. The show we're most looking forward to is happening tomorrow afternoon at 2pm. It's your time to shine with our fortnightly talent show. We've been taking auditions all week but fear not, we've saved a couple of spots for you guys, so if you want to enter, we're holding auditions right here after your welcome event. Everyone is welcome!"

Tracey gave me a look, raising her eyebrows and giving a nod, as if to ask if I was interested in taking part. I shook my head in response.

Tammy high-fived Tommy, passing the limelight back to him. "Do we have any tossers in the room?" He asked, smirking.

Whilst most people stared blankly and with confused expressions, the guy in the Speedos enthusiastically shouted out, "Hell yeah!"

Tammy added, "Our daytime activities include Bean Bag Bowls - where you'll put your tossing talents to good use. We also hope to see you taking part in our afternoon quizzes, water polo and more! The full entertainment timetable can be found in reception."

Tommy jumped back in enthusiastically with the announcement, "And we've saved the best news for last! This weekend we are joined by the internet sensation, Lee Lauren!"

For the first time since the duo began this uncomfortable act, the audience perked up with sounds of excitement coming mostly from children and teenagers - Tracey included, of course.

The Speedo guy took this opportunity to shout, "Titties!" It became increasingly apparent that he had zero self-awareness of how to appropriately act at a family venue.

I glanced over towards Lee, who looked extremely smug off the back of the reaction given to the mere mention of his name.

Seriously, how did a guy like him get a girl like Alizia?

Tommy waited for the crowd to settle before continuing, "You're no doubt already aware that Lee Lauren will be shooting an advert for us, which will hopefully overshadow the whole... diarrhoea thing. You may be wondering if Lee Lauren is happy to speak to his fans whilst he's here. Well, we have an official statement from his agent. It says..."

Tommy pulled a piece of paper from his pocket before reading aloud, "Lee Lauren knows he wouldn't be as phenomenally successful as he is without the love and support from his fans. Therefore, he is more than happy to talk to these fans, sign autographs and pose for pictures... all for the reasonable fee of twenty pounds per request - of which, a percentage will go to his founding charity, 'Underappreciated Geniuses'. The charity pays the rent, utilities and expenses of young talent, allowing them to focus on their online content full time as opposed to wasting time in a demenial and common 9-5 job."

Tammy concluded, "Exciting stuff! We're very lucky to have him here. Now... before we finish up, we have a few important health and safety announcements to make-"

"Nobody cares," interrupted a loud voice. You can probably guess whose. It would seem the Speedo guy was right though, because almost everyone had now begun to grab their belongings and started to leave.

Chapter Four: The Audition - Aiden's Story

Before starting what I'd hoped would be a lazy few hours of lounging and writing, I rushed to get my own notepad and, of course, a change of t-shirt. I opted for a simple black v neck top without any declaration of being a princess.

I collapsed on a sun lounger between Dad and Uncle Dave, with Tracey a few spaces across from me and an empty space where Mum would have been if she weren't off doing God knows what with God knows who.

Credit to my Uncle, who had once again got us a fantastic spot, close to the pool. It was thankfully far enough away from where The Taylor Twins held most of their activities, so I was grateful we wouldn't hear them - well, not as loudly. Bliss. There's only so many times you can hear, "Awesome job, buddy," before the twitching commences, unable to withstand the repetitious droning.

Uncle Dave has this surprisingly genius way of convincing people to give up their own sun loungers for us to use. He'll boldly approach someone and say with enormous conviction and no shame, "I'm sorry, I was hoping we could take your spot... because of my bowel movements." After trialling a whole host of peculiar excuses throughout the years, this was the only one that raised no further questions.

After shimmying myself into a comfortable position on the lounger, a sight ahead of me completely caught me off-guard.

My heart started to race.

In the distance was a tall block of flats. It was almost identical to the building that had been haunting my dreams - yes, the one I had leapt from so many times. Perhaps this structure had implanted itself into my subconscious mind once discussions of coming here had begun?

I think Uncle Dave became attuned to the situation. With empathy not being 'his thing', I was surprised he'd picked up on it actually. He looked at the block of flats and then towards me in a concerned manner. I braced myself for what I expected to be a speech focused on my well-being. What he actually said was, "Imagine being so rich that you don't have to worry how much a Freddo costs. You could literally grab a box full of those chocolate frogs like it was nothing."

The more predictable Uncle Dave was back in the room.

".... Right," I replied - confused but quite relieved that the conversation hadn't gone in the direction I'd feared. "What makes you say that?"

"That guy going around in the t-shirt with his own face on it... Lee Lauren? Tracey was showing me how rich he is and it's mental money! The guy even has a tattoo with real gold mixed into the ink."

"Of course he does," I muttered under my breath. "Look, if you don't mind, I've got some writing to do."

"Say no more. As do I."

Unsurprisingly, Uncle Dave didn't last thirty seconds before continuing, "What are you writing?"

I figured I had nothing to lose by being honest. "I'm giving song writing another go. I'm hoping to have written one by the end of this weekend."

"Good on you. Yeah... I reckon I could write a hit song."

"Yes, I remember you saying so after we listened to that Beyoncé song on the radio the other day."

"Seriously, 90% of that song was five words repeated over and over - Who run the world? Girls." He continued, "Here's three even better words... bacon flavoured titties. Put a decent beat behind it and you've got a guaranteed hit."

"I think you're missing the point. As repetitive as it is, her song is about female empowerment. Unless I'm not picking up on some kind of subtle hidden message beneath the surface, your song appears to be about nothing more than titties that are bacon flavoured."

Uncle Dave looked insulted before an attempt to defend himself. "Erm, hello? My book is literally all about female empowerment. Let me read you a chapt-"

"I'm good," I interrupted. "I'd rather just concentrate on my own stuff if you don't mind?"

"Say no more. Sorry."

I took a deep breath, hoping to reboot my brain from thoughts of frogs and porn - not linked.

Within moments of putting pen to paper, I recoiled, as water started squirting on my face.

"Seriously?" I screamed furiously. "What now?"

As I wiped the liquid from my eyes, a young boy slowly came into focus. The brat, who couldn't have been older than ten-years-old, towered over me with a large water pistol.

He shot me once more, before sinisterly laughing and scurrying away - presumably to find his next victim.

I took another deep breath, desperately trying to compose myself.

Tracey then gave out a shriek.

"What?" I screamed, growing even more frustrated than before.

"Lee Lauren has posted that he'll be judging the talent show, tomorrow" she said excitedly. "He's literally at the auditions right now. Aiden, please can we go? Please? Please?"

I couldn't think of anything worse.

"Look. Everyone. Can you just let me relax and get some writing done?" I pleaded. "Tracey, go without me."

"I don't want to go on my own."

Tracey looked at Uncle Dave with pathetic, but the most effective puppy eyes she'd mastered over time. "Don't look at me either," he said. "Like your brother, I've got to crack on with some writing too."

I looked away from Tracey, trying to avoid the inevitable disheartened gaze. Instead, I got that very look from Dad. "Has it occurred to you that what might be an hour of slight annoyance for you could be the best hour of your sisters' life," he whispered. "You know how much this would mean to her."

I took a genuine moment to consider it before replying, "I'm sorry. What I'm trying to work on right now is more important."

Out of nowhere, Uncle Dave asked out loud, "Does the word pegging have one 'g' or two?"

"Red card," shouted the family in unison.

I knew that my writing simply wasn't going to be completed or even started in the presence of my family - Uncle Dave in particular.

"Let's go, Tracey," I urged her. She responded with what was fast becoming her trademark squeal.

I figured that I could attempt the writing again once I was on my own - perhaps after doing my sister this quick, and I mean quick, favour. I did not plan to be in the presence of Lee any longer than I needed to be.

Heading towards our destination, I could see the little brat who had cowardly blindsided me with his water gun. He was stood at the side of the pool, attacking more unsuspecting families with his weapon. He was on a rampage.

I took the opportunity to release some of my stress by nudging him into the pool as we crossed paths. "Piss off," I said softly whilst making contact.

"Sorry... accident," I proceeded to shout unconvincingly for the benefit of the onlookers that had been terrorised just moments earlier.

A handful of them gratefully smiled at me. I triumphantly smiled back. I dare say there may have been a slow clap started in my honour if it weren't for the moment being ruined by a concerned voice shouting, "The kid is drowning!"

How was I supposed to know that the brat couldn't swim?

"Let's go. Quicker," I said trying to hurry Tracey along.

I would like to stress that I'm not a monster. I was not leaving the scene of a crime as there simply was no crime. There must have been a dozen, if not more, adults jumping in for the boy. He was perfectly fine.

Tracey picked up more speed as we drew closer to the entertainment hall. She was moving in a way where she was clearly excited and keen, whilst also trying to look composed and cool. I didn't have the heart to tell her this but in all honesty, it looked like she was trying to hold in a turd.

Speaking of which, when Tracey pleaded for us to sit as close to Lee as possible, I guided us to a table beside his and knew exactly what to say to clear a space. I leant in to some random couple and whispered, "I'm sorry, I was hoping we could take your spot... because of my bowel movements." They gave me a look of both disgust and confusion but lo and behold, it had worked again.

Within reaching distance, there they were - Lee and Alizia.

Tracey was practically hyperventilating being so close to her idol. I'd have insulted her on the way she was gawping if it weren't for the fact that I recently learnt this was an unfortunate, hereditary trait.

From the comfort of his seat, Lee picked up a radio mic and announced, "Auditioning next is Albert Barns, who will be doing some stand-up comedy for us."

Up on the stage walked 'Speedo guy' - not that most of the room would even have any awareness of this because, like Tracey, they couldn't stop goggling their internet hero.

Proudly sporting the tiny swimsuit, Albert grabbed a second microphone placed centre-stage and shouted, "Titties."

The audience howled like it wasn't the fiftieth time they'd heard it that day.

"Brilliant - I like your style," Lee stated. "But I must remind you that this will be a family show. Is the rest of your material family-friendly?"

The newly flustered man pulled out cue cards from inside of his speedos. I gagged when it entered my mind what they may have smelt like. The guy frantically flicked through the cards, clearly struggling to find some jokes that were suitable.

He shrugged before asking, "What if, instead of titties, I shout breasts?"

"Here's my honest opinion. You already look like a sex offender. Maybe don't go out of your way to sound like one."

The audience howled at Lee's brutal feedback. "It's a no from me," he continued attempting his best Simon-Cowell impersonation.

Albert exited the stage disheartened and Lee wasted no time in getting the next act up. "Seven-year-old Lucy Parks... you're up."

The young girls' parents encouraged the visibly anxious child onto the stage. She looked truly terrified.

Lee made no effort to put this kid at ease, instead demanding, "Play her music. Let's do this!"

Although blatantly nervous, Lucy started to perform the simplest but cutest dance routine. Her parents looked so proud, her father even wiping away a tear.

Young Lucy can't have even been a minute into the performance before the obnoxious judge raised his hand - signalling for the music to stop.

Lucy looked towards her parents, confused. The room was now so silent; you'd have literally heard a pin drop. It seemed everyone was desperate to hear why the child had been interrupted so quickly.

Lee seemed to be taking a moment to gather his thoughts. "Sweetie... I'm just wondering if the dance gets any better?"

The poor girl, who now understandably seemed more nervous than before, took a moment to think before hopefully throwing her body into a forward roll.

Confirming to me that Lee was the monster I'd assumed he was, the judge continued, "If that's the best dance move you have... you're not ready."

You could see the awkwardness planted over almost everyone's faces. Her parents' expression conveyed to me they were angry at Lee. Understandably so.

"Who told you that you can dance, Lucy?" Lee asked.

She pointed towards her mum and dad.

Lee took the Simon Cowell impersonation further, telling this confused child, "Your parents are what we call 'enablers'. As they're not going to tell you that you cannot dance, I feel it's my duty to do so."

In the corner of my eye, I caught Alizia give her partner a subtle kick - expressing her, and everyone else's disbelief.

"But... you're cute," Lee offered reluctantly. "People like cute... so, I guess you're in."

The audience gave a half-hearted clap - perhaps still slightly shocked by what they had just witnessed.

The now disgruntled man-child yelped, "Let's get this over with. Last on my list is a young man - just eleven years old. Let's hope a few more years of practice time makes all the difference. Give it up for... Lil Problemz."

Confidently skipping onto the stage came the next auditionee. "What's up," the boy screamed into the mic.

Lee continued to lead the auditions, asking "What's with the name, Lil Problemz?"

"It's my rapper name."

"So, you aspire to be the next Machine Gun Kelly? Eminem perhaps?"

"Nah, I don't relate to their lyrics. I don't relate to any other rappers out there. But just because I don't have girls or fast cars, it doesn't mean I don't have things to say."

"Well, I for one am very intrigued to hear what you have to say. Go for it."

As a beat played over the speakers, Lil Problemz boldly paraded around the stage.

"I wanna play Xbox Mum,
So why you trippin?
Go get better WiFi,
Cos my shoot-em-up keeps skipping.
It's just me in my squad, not getting in a hit.
Is it cos I suck? No!
It's cos our internet is shi-"

"Okay, great," Lee quickly chirped in. "I'll need to look over your lyrics prior to tomorrow's show. As long as the words are appropriate enough, consider yourself in. In fact, we should chat properly soon because you're exactly the kind of person I look to enrol in my 'Underappreciated Geniuses' programme."

Lil Problemz gave a big, smug smile before emphasising his "bad boy" image with a literal mic drop.

A more mature female voice shouted from across the room, "Pick up that microphone, young man!"

The boy sheepishly did as he was told.

The mysterious woman, who I can only assume was his mother, continued to shout, "Now, apologise to the people that paid good money for that microphone."

"Sorry," he said with a much more submissive tone than we'd just heard within his rap and looking rather embarrassed by the situation."

Lee announced to the room, "Last chance for anyone wanting to audition."

I leant towards Tracey and begrudgingly explained, "If you really want to meet this guy, now is your chance. Go audition."

"I have no talent though," she replied disheartened. "The only thing I'm good at is annoying you."

My sister gave me that look as if a lightbulb had just lit up in her mind. "You're the singer," she continued enthusiastically. "Just go up on that stage... sing one song... get through to the show... introduce me to Lee Lauren backstage... Lee Lauren then changes my life... I buy you a house."

I looked at Tracey in disbelief before stating, "That's clearly a well thought-through plan but there's not a chance I'm going up on that stage."

You know in movies, when a character will state that they won't do a certain thing before cutting to the next scene, where they're then doing that very thing? I'm ashamed to say that's exactly what happened in this particular situation. How did Tracey convince me to do something I was totally adamant I was not going to do? After frantically scrolling through her phone, she slid a social media post in front of me. It was an old tweet from Alizia stating, "There is nothing sexier than a guy that can play guitar and sing well."

I'd love to have said that I couldn't be so easily manipulated into doing something but it is what it is. Upon reading that tweet, with zero hesitation I called out, "I have a song."

All eyes were suddenly on me.

Instant regret.

"I... I have a song but I don't have my guitar with me," I added much more timidly.

Lee looked at me with what I can only describe as a scheming pantomime-esque smirk.

"I recognise you," he said on his mic for all to hear. "I see you took your princess t-shirt off."

"I see you kept yours on," I teased, whilst metaphorically cementing that line into my top ten list of burns. He did not look amused. Surprisingly, his fiancé did. Although subtle, Alizia was definitely smirking before kindly suggesting, "You can borrow my guitar, if you want to."

She drew my attention to a guitar leant on their table. The fact that she owned one made her even more perfect. It was a gesture that was very much appreciated but at this point, enough time had passed to realise what a horrible situation I had put myself in.

I was about to decline the kind offer when Tracey took my hand and comfortingly said, "If you need a distraction this weekend... this is it." Many would argue that this comment was nothing more than manipulation but I know my sister and could tell it was actually rather sincere.

Taking a deep breath to compose myself, I got up and strolled over to Alizia. "I'd love to borrow your guitar, thank you," I said in a voice several decibels lower than usual. It was an attempt to make myself sound cooler but it came out more like a terrible Arnold Schwarzenegger impression.

"Just don't finish your act the same way that Lil Problemz did," Alizia joked before handing me what I sensed was her prized possession - one that, for whatever reason, she trusted me with.

Growing increasingly infuriated by the situation unfolding before him, Lee demanded, "Go grab the mic and tell us your name, age and song title."

Walking towards the stage and seeing all the people in the crowd, once again invoked memories of better times that now began flooding through my mind. When my old bandmates and I performed, we felt invincible for a solid ninety minutes. It didn't even matter if we were performing to a bad crowd - we were in our own bubble and nothing outside of it mattered.

It dawned on me that I actually had no idea what song I was going to sing.

The titles of my last few creations were, 'Bleeding to Feel Again', 'Sweet Dreams Forever' and 'Fuck off Talking About Freddo'. You probably guessed that none of these options would be suitable for children.

I tried to force the perfect song to the forefront of my mind and thank God, it eventually did. I hadn't thought about this piece for the longest time.

"My name is Aiden, I'm seventeen and this is a song I wrote called 'I Want to Bake a Cookie With You'."

"Sounds creepy. Can you maybe perform a cover?" Lee sighed whilst rolling his eyes.

"I can't, no."

"To be honest with you, original songs are pretty boring. People want to hear tracks that they recognise and can therefore sing along to. I'm pretty sure everyone here would agree."

Of course, most of the audience did indeed agree with their idol, nodding away. Lee literally could have said, "All music is the devil so drink my Kool-Aid to cleanse your sins," and the crowd wouldn't have hesitated to drink that poison. Quite worrying, really.

Lee's mic picked up Alizia whispering to her partner. I've no idea what was said exactly but he seemed to be aggravated by it.

"Just sing your damn song," he demanded.

All I had to do was strum the first chord and I was back in my comfort bubble and ready to play on.

"I want to bake a cookie with you,
There's nothing else I'd rather do.
In the time it takes to make it, perhaps I'll admit,
I want a cookie but I also want you too.
When you are gone, I'm so incomplete.

The world around me so obsolete.
This is something that I had to say,
And it may make you want to run away,
But at least I'll have a delicious treat to eat.
So do you want to bake a cookie with me?
Why not start and then you'll see,
the world will smell so sweeter,
our lives so much completer,
and it all started with you and me and...
quite likely... a burnt cookie."

The audience reacted really well to the song, applauding delightedly. It was a sound I had enormously missed. I didn't realise just how much until now.

The one person who didn't clap was Lee. Expressionless, he picked up his mic and stated, "I didn't like it. I can't eat cookies as I'm diabetic – you may have seen one of my five videos about it. Try and be a little bit more sensitive next time."

His level of self-entitlement was unbelievable.

Lee and Alizia begun having a quiet but most definitely heated debate. After a few muffled sentences I could just about hear her say, "Put him through."

Lee looked at me with a piercing stare before announcing, "I guess I'm just not your demographic. The song sounds like it was written by a small child or a mentally challenged adult."

Looking at the disappointment all over Alizia's face, Lee heatedly concluded, "But... you're through. Whatever. As for everyone else confirmed to perform tomorrow, you have exactly ten minutes to see me at the side of the stage. If you are performing to a song, you need to give me that track now. When I give you the order of which you'll be performing, make a note of it as I shall only tell you once. If you want a photo, have your money ready."

I headed back towards my seat, pushing past a wave of excited children who were rushing towards the stage, queuing up to see Lee - who, unsurprisingly, had aggressively barged his way past me.

I handed back Alizia her guitar.

Perhaps it was wishful thinking on my part but I felt like she looked me dead in the eyes for a good second - maybe even two. It was definitely longer than what would typically be considered the standard amount of time for holding eye contact.

She said nothing however and so, I quietly returned to my seat.

Tracey looked towards me excited, but also rather panicked. "You'll do the show tomorrow, right? You are literally my key to getting closer to Lee Lauren."

"Yes, I shall do the show" I replied reluctantly.

"Well then... you need to be in that queue. Go. Go talk to Lee Lauren."

"Or... take this opportunity to go speak to him yourself and get the info on my behalf."

Tracey was already five steps away within a flash of a second before turning back to shout, "Thank you!"

She suddenly spun around, marched back towards me and practically begged, "Can I borrow twenty pounds?"

I knew why she wanted my money and so I shook my head and explained, "The thought of giving that guy a single penny of mine makes me feel physically sick."

Her face dropped.

In that moment, I could picture the disapproving look that my dad would be giving me. "However," I continued whilst pulling out my wallet. "The joy I know this photo would bring you means more to me."

She swiped the note faster than... faster than something that moves real fast. Goddammit, I needed to get those creative juices flowing again if I was ever going to complete my song!

Over the commotion of excited kids, I could just about make out the sound of my cookie song being whistled.

I looked over to see Alizia sat there, staring directly towards me, whistling away. She gave me a smile and nod that, to me, said, "Good job."

I felt like I was at a crossroad. Her first impression of me can't have been great, to say the least, but I felt like I'd redeemed myself with the cute cookie song. I knew that whatever happened next would play a crucial role in influencing her overall thoughts of me moving forward.

I also knew that the more I thought about the situation, the more likely I'd be to talk myself out of doing something – or doing anything.

With very little thought put into what I would say, I sat myself down onto the seat that Lee's ass had been on, just moments just ago – an item that I dare say could be sold on eBay to some nutter hoping to get just a whiff of their idols backside. I figured that would be the typical behaviour of people in this modern world.

Alizia gave me a confused look that screamed, "What is happening here?"

"Interesting fact about Dave Grohl," I said, surprisingly confident. "Before Foo Fighters, he started a band with his sister. Short lived, of course. My sister wanted to start a band with me too but... no chance."

Alizia stared blankly at me for a few moments before flatly stating, "Interesting fact about me... I don't care."

My heart shattered immediately. I could feel an anxiety attack slowly building up inside me and knew I had to evacuate the situation as soon as possible. As I stood up Alizia burst out laughing. "I'm totally kidding," she said.

I was not amused.

I sat back down like I was in an awkward game of musical chairs. "That was really mean," I said, whilst silently, my own inner dialogue attempted to analyse the situation. *Am I talking to the female equivalent of Lee Lauren? Is this angel, in fact, the devil?* I'd no idea.

"I'm sorry," she said sincerely. "I saw the joke and I just went with it."

"Okay. It's all good," I replied as my heartrate slowly returned to a normal beat.

"So, why not start a band with your sister? It could be fun."

Starting afresh, I explained, "It's not that she wants to be in a band. She just wants to be famous. She doesn't care what she becomes famous for - she just wants the fans, the money and the big house."

"Good on her. Most people want that."

I heard Lee Lauren give out an exaggerated laugh. I couldn't help but feel this was for my benefit - a little reminder that he was close by and watching. Either way, I chose to not react and carried on with the conversation. "That's one of the reasons why I hate this world," I said.

I couldn't control these rants anymore. They were like a tic and so I went on. "Nobody seems to aspire to put in the hard work these days. They see that it takes ten to fourteen years to become a fully licensed doctor and they think screw that - we can prat about on camera for ten to fourteen seconds and potentially earn from that one video what these medical professionals earn in one year. When we went through a worldwide pandemic, there was a beautiful moment of time hidden amongst the horror where we were finally giving credit to those that had once been looked down on. The people that stocked the shelves in our supermarkets, those that drove the trucks and the underpaid carers working tirelessly in retirement homes - finally, we were screaming about them from the rooftops. They were the ones all over social media. Just when I thought there might be hope for society, lockdown restrictions were lifted and within mere minutes, a picture popped up on my timeline with some newspaper saying here's a photo of a famous singer... and he's drinking a coffee - like the world was begging to see this shit again. The sad thing is, I think it was."

Alizia looked me dead in the eyes, puzzled. "How old are you?" she asked.

"I'm seventeen."

"No offence, but you sound seventy."

"I know," I said with a smirk. "I feel it sometimes. Changing the subject, I assume you having your guitar means you're performing in the talent show tomorrow too?"

"Actually, no. It's a comfort thing. I feel... less anxious with it in hand or by my side. It would be more convenient if something a little lighter and easier to carry gave me the same level of comfort, but it is what it-."

Our conversation was interrupted by Tracey shrieking whilst taking a selfie with that dickhead.

I looked over and shook my head. Apparently, I hadn't hidden my annoyance towards the guy very well. "You're not a fan of Lee Lauren, I'm guessing?" Alizia said.

Right on cue, Lee shouted out loud, "I'm done. I need a sandwich. Please... everyone... shoo!"

"What? How could I not be a fan of the wonderfully charming Lee Lauren," I said sarcastically.

"From your perspective, I get it. I see a different side to him though. He's just a scared boy out of his comfort zone, playing the game before it comes to an inevitable end."

He didn't look in the least bit scared to me as he started marching over towards us. Tracey following closely behind him, of course.

Lee ended up standing so close to me that - and I wish I was exaggerating - his crotch was less than half an inch away from me - perfectly level to my eye line. I never thought I'd ever say this but from what I could see from the outline, his penis looked majestic. Of course it did - and he clearly knew it. This jerk was most definitely peacocking me again. No pun intended.

"Babes, I'm gonna get a quick snack before we shoot this advert," Lee said to Alizia - with his genitals jiggling, rhythmically right in my face with each word he spoke.

Tracey took a deep breath before declaring excitedly, "Lee Lauren said I can come and watch him shoot the advert and he's going to give me advice on my own channel!"

"Really?" I asked, confused by this revelation.

Lee explained, "Alizia don't like being dragged to these work events so I may as well take someone that'll appreciate it."

Out of politeness, I'd usually look into the eyes of anyone talking to me. On this occasion I did not - genuinely concerned that the slightest movement of my head could lead to actual physical contact with the beast lurking inside his pants.

Lee continued, "I like to do nice things for the fans from time to time."

After leaning in to give his fiancé a kiss, Lee concluded, "I'll see you at the beach party afterwards, babes. 8pm. Don't be late."

Something didn't feel right about my sister hanging out with this guy, but who was I to object to Tracey living out her literal dream? I had to take comfort in Alizia's comment that maybe he wasn't a massive dic... idiot. A massive idiot.

"Have fun," I said reluctantly.

Alizia chirped in, "Aiden and I will be having our own fun, won't we?"

"*You know it, babes,*" is what I desperately wanted to say. What actually came out was a nervous laugh - pretty much identical to none other than Disney's Goofy.

She continued, "We're gonna go check out the Dynamite Diving Board, aren't we?"

Not wanting to risk a repeat of my voice box malfunction, I simply nodded along. I think I may have been in shock that Alizia wanted to hang out with me. Or... was I actually a pawn in some mind game designed to make Lee jealous?

Meh, I didn't particularly care. Either way, I would get to spend more time with the most beautiful person I'd ever laid eyes on.

If Alizia was trying to make her fiancé jealous however, I sensed it was working. Without even seeing Lee's eyes, I knew they were staring right at me. I could feel it.

"You know what," Lee said sternly. "That's actually great to hear. There's a lot of proper manly men roaming around Happys. I'd much rather my girl was hanging out with someone like you than someone like them."

I probably should have been offended by this comment, but again... meh. I was getting to spend more time with Alizia and that's all that mattered to me now.

My crush looked at me with a cheeky smirk before asking, "You think you can handle the Dynamite Diving Board?"

I opted once more for nodding, in affirmation.

Of course I could handle it. With Alizia by my side, I felt like I'd be able to handle anything.

Chapter Five: The Dynamite Diving Board - Aiden's Story

As it turned out, I could not handle the Dynamite Diving Board.

Stood upon the edge of the very top of it, my entire body froze. I was literally scared stiff.

I looked down in horror as Alizia enthusiastically cheered for me to jump.

I once again saw flashes of my reoccurring dream in my mind and I clung on to the side railings as if my life depended on it. Much like in that dream, a crowd had begun to form below me, once it had become apparent that a dramatic situation was unfolding. I think it's fair to say that the majority of Brits love nothing more than a bit of drama. Some of our country's most popular television shows focus around people suffering physical or psychological harm.

Although Alizia was at quite a distance below me, I could still see that she was becoming increasingly mortified by the situation. Despite her embarrassment of being associated with the wimp on the diving board, she still had the heart to shout unconfidently.

"You've got this, Aiden. You just have to jump!"

"Oh, that's how this works," I muttered frustrated. Like I had no grasp on the concept of how a bloody diving board worked!

I'd like to stress that I know Alizia was trying to help. I was just so annoyed - predominantly, with myself.

I could see Tommy Taylor from the entertainments team march towards the crowd with his trusted megaphone. "You've got this, kid," he bellowed, alerting anyone within hearing distance. "You just have to jump!"

Seriously?

Maybe their advice had something to it though. Perhaps I'd been overthinking the situation and all I needed to do was... well, fall.

Just one single leap of faith, or even a simple flop and maybe, just maybe, it would be enough to compensate for Alizia's first impression of me in my Princess t-shirt.

I had to do it now.

I confidently unleashed my tight grip on the bars, stood majestically at the edge of the board, looked down and... nope, it wasn't going to happen. I reluctantly admitted defeat and headed back towards the ladder, tail between my legs.

I was horrified that a long queue of children had formed whilst I'd been faffing about. There was no way I'd be able to squeeze past them all, let alone face the shame of not finding the courage to jump, when these kids, half my age, were about to do so, fearlessly.

Tommy once again took to his megaphone. "This is a public announcement," he said. "Please note that Lee Lauren will be here filming in just a few minutes. If you do not want to be filmed in the background, please leave now. I also ask that you do not harass the talent for photos at this time as he is on a tight schedule."

That was exactly what I needed to hear. There was no way I was going to give that dickhead the pleasure of seeing me stuck up here.

I turned and began to run the short distance of the boards' surface. I think I'd have committed myself to the dive this time if it weren't for a whistle being blown authoritatively, mid-sprint. Knowing the lifeguard had likely blown this as a warning not to run, I panicked. I was mid leap, feet off the ground, when simultaneously, my body spun and I manically clung onto the edge. I was just hanging there, much like the rock-climbing scene in Mission Impossible - except I don't recall Tom Cruise starting to cry during that scene.

I could hear laughs from below - all justified, of course. I was an embarrassment.

I had two choices here. I could use every ounce of what little upper-body strength I had left or I could let go and allow myself to fall.

The decision was soon taken out of my hands as a child slowly headed towards me. It was just my luck that It was the brat that I had technically left to drown earlier in the day.

He edged closer with his water gun aimed directly towards my face. This kid was out for revenge and his smug grin cemented my fate.

"I'm sorry," I said with tears now racing down my cheeks.

"Piss off," he echoed my earlier instruction sinisterly, whilst pulling back the trigger.

I screamed whilst plummeting towards the water. I would later find out that the sound I had produced led to numerous concerned guests reporting to reception that they were hearing the wails of a distressed woman.

The next few moments that followed were a blur. I don't even remember making impact with the water. I'm not sure if I passed out or not, but before I knew it, I was collapsed on the floor beside the pool with a crowd of spectators huddled around me. One of those people was the lifeguard. "Are you okay?" he asked concernedly.

"I think so," I croaked.

"I'm going to take that as a 'yes' because my shift ended like two minutes ago," he hurriedly declared before carefully sprinting off across the wet and slippery ground.

Tommy Taylor looked relieved too. "You're alive. Thank god. Last thing we need right now is more bad press."

The crowd quickly dispersed upon the disappointing revelation that I was doing fine. The one person that stayed, to my surprise, was Alizia. I was almost certain she'd have vacated long before now. I would not have blamed her for doing so.

She had a look written across her face that screamed, "*I've no idea what to say right now.*"

Pathetically, I looked at her and cried, "That was really embarrassing, wasn't it?"

"I mean; it wasn't... not embarrassing. Especially as you've shit yourself."

"Oh come on," I sighed, truly mortified. "I really am turning into my Uncle Dave."

Alizia stared silently for a few uncomfortable seconds before bursting out laughing. "You're fine," she said. "To my knowledge, your swimming shorts are shit-free."

"Unlike your jokes, which are... kind of mean," I said mostly tongue-in-cheek.

We made our way to some nearby sun loungers - giving me the perfect opportunity to embarrass myself even further. It was inevitable, I was realising.

As I fought to regulate my breathing, I could hear an excited commotion from all around. Although I couldn't see the source of the sudden mania, I could certainly guess who it was aimed at.

Yup, of course, there he was.

Lee began climbing his way up to the top board that I had utterly humiliated myself on. He was so confident in doing so. I wanted nothing more than for him to crumble once he reached the top, just as I had. Of course, he wasn't even phased. Without a smidgen of hesitation, he elegantly made his dive. I don't think I've even seen

Olympians diving so gracefully and his camera crew, his fiancé, my sister and many adoring young fans were all there to witness it - all stood in awe before applauding him.

I seemed to be the only person who was not taken in by this guy. I felt like I was stuck in the most horrible nightmare. I think I actually preferred the one where I was falling to my own death.

Just two feet in front of Alizia and I, Lee soon emerged from the water. He was now close enough for me to see his chiselled 8-pack of abs. I didn't even know that was a thing until now.

Alizia proudly shouted, "Great job, baby."

He smugly replied, "It wasn't too bad for my first ever attempt at diving."

"Oh, come on!" I shouted out loud. *Shit.* It had been my intention to think these words internally, but as was becoming the trend, my mouth betrayed me.

Lee seemed to take great pleasure in knowing he'd gotten a rise out me. Smugly, he explained, "You're essentially just jumping into water so I figured how hard can it be? Not that hard at all as it turns out."

He turned his focus towards Alizia before continuing, "Remember... beach party... 8pm. Don't be late."

In a flash, he was gone with his entourage - my sister included - following closely behind like a flock of sheep.

Alizia and I lay back on our sun loungers. She turned to ask, "So, Aiden, who is the cookie song for?"

I perhaps should have taken a moment to choose my words more wisely before declaring, "The most amazing and gorgeous twelve-year-old."

I only twigged how dodgy that sounded upon seeing the sudden look of horror on Alizia's face.

"Let me word that better," I panicked.

I was desperately trying to choose my next few words more wisely when my topless Uncle appeared out of nowhere. Great timing, as always.

"Oh, hey Aiden," he said in a really over-the-top school drama-esque voice.

I instantly knew where this was going. He was about to follow through with this wingman malarkey he'd been chatting to me about the day before.

"As I was putting your luggage bag in your room, a few bits fell out," the facade continued. "If my memory serves me right, there was your book of poetry, which represents your sensitive side. There was a whole bunch of out-of-date Freddo's, which represents how you like to live dangerously and not short of a few quid. And there was a pack of magnum sized condoms, which represents your huge-"

"Red card! Leave," I demanded.

"Okay," he sighed defensively. Before departing, he inappropriately gawped at Alizia and proceeded to give me an animated and approving wink.

"You know she can see you winking, right?" I said pained by my Uncle's lack of discretion.

"Sorry," he whispered whilst winking with the other eye - just as blatantly.

As Uncle Dave began to walk away, I wasted no time in continuing to stress, "Anyway, as I was trying to say... I do not fancy a twelve-year-old!"

My Uncle was clearly still close enough to hear this as he turned and looked at me with confusion and horror.

"I wrote the cookie song when I was twelve... for a girl who, at the time, was also twelve," I explained in a rushed panic. "We were... still are... the same age."

Alizia shook her head in disgust before laughing and mimicking my Uncle's cheeky wink.

Much like her fiancé, she seemed to enjoy watching me get flustered - but not in the same way - I hoped. With Alizia, it seemed much more playful. Either that or I was being naïve, which was fairly typical for me, actually.

"And where is this girl now?" Alizia asked.

"Probably baking cookies with someone else. After our play date I wrote her a letter declaring my love for her and she thought it would be funny to read it out loud to our class. They all found it so hilarious. I no longer fancied her after that."

"That sounds brutal."

"It was. I wrote a follow up song called 'You Can Shove Those Cookies Up Your Arse' but it didn't feel appropriate singing that one at the audition." I gave out a pitiful laugh before adding, "It's funny now, I guess. You're probably thinking what can a kid possibly know about love and relationships at such a young age?"

"Not at all. Breakups are so much more painful at a young age. You don't have the life experience to know that time will eventually heal the heart and that things will, at some point, start to get better. It's a really difficult time."

"Exactly," I agreed, excitedly, upon discovering that we shared this similar outlook on life.

Alizia asked, "The 'magnum condom guy' is your Uncle Dave, I assume?"

"Yes. I'm so glad he was able to join us on this weekend," I said sarcastically. "He means well but has no filter and very little self-awareness. I remember he was once shown a photo of a young boy by a proud mother, at which point my Uncle explained that the child had looks that Hitler would have approved of. This was apparently a compliment."

"Well, damn," Alizia laughed awkwardly. "What's with his blacked out tattoos?"

"It's an unfortunate situation," I smirked. "He got himself a 70s to 90s pop culture tattoo - featuring all of his favourite people from film and television. Through the years, one by one, these former celebrities were shamed for numerous terrible crimes. Each time this happened, he wasted no time in having their faces blacked out. Ironically, it's a tattoo artist named Jim that fixes it."

"You know people will still be offended by his tattoos, right? The cover-ups now look like black faces."

I hadn't really thought of it like that until now. "They really do," I cringed. "And of course, people will make that assumption and get pissed off as opposed to actually asking for the context behind it. Context is literally everything and yet people rarely want to hear it because more so than not, the truth is far less interesting. That's one of the reasons why I hate this world. We're all-"

"Okay, what is this rant thing you've got going on?" Alizia interrupted, teasingly.

I took a moment to consider my answer. "I... genuinely don't know," I said. "Old habits die hard, I guess."

"You're sure you're seventeen, right?"

"Yes," I sniggered.

"What happened to you to make you see the world through the eyes of some really old guy that has been battered and bruised throughout his entire life? Fill me in on the context of that behaviour."

I knew the answer to this question but I wasn't going to tell her. I still wasn't ready to talk about it. Whilst conducting a lie in my mind, Alizia broke the silence by explaining, "If ranting and raving about the shitty things in this world makes you genuinely happy - you go for it. Own it. It just seems... it seems like it must be so draining. It's a shame that someone of our age wouldn't rather zone that energy into something more positive."

"You're right," I admitted. "I don't actually like being this way and I wish you could have seen me a couple of years back. I was so different."

Alizia smiled in the way the Grinch did as he stole Christmas. She clearly had a plan.

"When was the last time you went to a party?"

"364 days ago."

"That's very precise," she giggled. "There's a beach party happening tonight for all the cast and crew involved in this advert that they're shooting. You should come."

"Is it going to be about all the cast and crew or is it actually going to be all about Lee?"

Alizia reluctantly gave a nod before agreeing, "You're right... it's going to be all about Lee Lauren. That's one of the reasons I'd love to see you there. You can keep me company whilst he basks in the attention of his adoring fans."

"You don't want to party with me," I muttered pathetically. "I don't even drink alcohol."

"Neither do I. Doesn't stop me being first on the dancefloor and letting my hair down."

Something was off. I was haunted by the fear it was possible I was being setup for a cruel or elaborate prank - like in the movie Carrie, where she's dowsed in pigs' blood.

"Come on. What's going on here?" I reluctantly pressed in an attempt to ease my anxieties. "Is this invite part of your dry humour? People like you don't choose to hang around with people like me without some kind of... agenda."

"People generalising based on looks and social status is one of the reasons why I hate this world," Alizia said playfully. "Look... I think you're weird."

I sat staring at Alizia, confused and rather offended.

She reassured me, "It's a compliment. You're the type of guy that wears a 'Mummy's little Princess' t-shirt. You auditioned for a talent show with a song you wrote about baking cookies. You were clearly terrified by that diving board... but you jumped regardless. It wasn't the smoothest of jumps - more of an overdramatic fall like Alan Rickman at the end of Die Hard - but you did it! You are refreshingly and wonderfully weird and it would be an honour to have you join me at the party."

I desperately wanted to tap into my inner cool after being given what was perhaps the best compliment of my life.

"Okay," I squeaked. *My damn mouth!*

Clearing my throat, I added, "I'll be there."

"One rule though... no rants if you can help it. I want you to at least try and enjoy yourself."

"Deal."

Whilst gathering her belongings, Alizia said, "Great - I look forward to seeing you at the beach directly opposite Happys at 8pm."

Best. Moment. Ever.

Chapter Six: "And so... I jumped." - Aiden's Story

I sat on the tiny bed, in my tiny bedroom, within the tiny caravan. However, for the first time in a long time, I didn't feel equally tiny. I felt big; important, like a King in his palace. I was on top of the world.

I placed my notepad in the drawer of my bedside table. It no longer bothered me whether I'd have this song written by the deadline I'd given myself. My priorities had changed. I had just been invited out by the most perfect girl and this is all I cared about now. Screw everything else.

It would be a good few hours until I'd see her face again and I just couldn't wait that long. I typed her name into YouTube and scrolled through the thumbnails of her videos, in true stalker fashion.

Tracey wasn't exaggerating when she boasted just how good Alizia was at transforming herself to appear to be a completely different person, using nothing but make-up. There was one image in particular where I thought, "*There is just no way this is her.*" The nose seemed rounder, the cheekbones thinner and there were wrinkles on her forehead that weren't there before. I clicked on the video and the sped-up footage confirmed the unbelievable transformation was for real.

Alizia had a natural talent and I was captivated.

I think I must have watched about twenty of her videos back to back before being interrupted by a knock at my door. I didn't mind. If anything, I was grateful that it prompted me to look at the time - which was later than I'd expected.

"Come in," I called out, gleefully.

My dad entered the room and upon seeing the big smile on my face, he teased, "What is happening? Aiden is smiling. It's a Happys miracle."

"I... feel good."

He sat beside me and softly explained, "I've missed that smile. That genuine, non-faking it smile." He continued, "I came to see what you're up to this evening."

"I'm going to be hanging out with a friend."

"A female friend?"

"Yes," I admitted, feeling my cheeks start to blush.

Dad gave a fatherly pat on my leg. "Just as I assumed. Good for you, kid," he said before getting up to leave the room.

"Dad," I called out urgently moments before he fully shut the door.

"What's up?"

"Obviously, I'm looking forward to hanging out with this girl tonight... but if there was a chance we could all hang out later as a family, like the old days, I'd choose that over anything and anyone else."

"I know," he croaked as tears filled his eyes.

I felt like this was my only chance to ask a question I'd been hesitant to bring up before now. "Does it not bother you knowing that Mum is out there with God knows who, doing who knows what?"

Dad looked deep in thought before replying, "No." Clearing his throat, he continued, "Things have been difficult for us all and each of us have our own way of dealing with things. I understand that it may look like she doesn't care, but she does. She cares a lot. She's pushing down the pain. It may not be the healthiest way to handle things but she'll get there when she's ready."

With that, he was gone.

I didn't have much time to process his words before there was another knock at my door - this time the speed of the knock sounded urgent.

I wasn't even given a chance to say, *"come in,"* before Uncle Dave stormed in. "Great job today - she's gorgeous," he said hurriedly. "Just checking... you're going to be heading out tonight, right? Making the most of your holiday? Say.... between the hours of 8 and 10pm?"

"I will be out then, yes," I replied suspiciously. "Everything okay?"

"Yeah, of course. I just thought it might be nice to have some 'me time' just to relax... read a book perhaps."

Unless the book in question involved seeking a man in a striped jumper named Wally, he was lying. I didn't question him any further though. Sometimes, ignorance is bliss - especially when the circumstances involve Uncle Dave.

"Well... enjoy whatever you end up doing. As I say, I won't be here," I repeated.

"Cool cool."

As Uncle Dave exited the room, I proceeded to pick out potential items of clothing that I could wear at the party. After going back and forth between the options for a while, I finally concluded which particular outfit would go down best with Alizia.

I confidently got back into my 'Mummy's Little Princess' t-shirt. Never before had I worn it so proudly.

I couldn't believe I was willingly going to a party. Not only that, but I was buzzing at the thought of it.

This feeling was immediately in danger of being short lived.

As I was about to leave the family caravan, I could hear Tracey sobbing from behind her bedroom door. A part of me wanted to peer in, to check on her. That would have been the right, brotherly, thing to do. I almost knocked but paused - my fist halting just an inch from her door. I couldn't do it. In my defence, it was obvious why she was upset. It would have been the same reason why we were all upset and I knew there was nothing I could say to her that hadn't already been repeated multiple times throughout the months we'd been attending our family counselling.

I figured there was little point in bringing both of our moods down and so, I reluctantly asked Uncle Dave to see to her before making my escape.

Upon arriving at the beach party, it quickly dawned on me that the mental image I'd created in my mind for how this would all look was a far cry from the reality unfolding before me.

I blame every American teen movie for my expectations of super toned youths, a mixologist flipping liquor bottles and perhaps a joyfully competitive game of football on the sand. What I saw were around twenty middle-aged smokers, a wheelie bin filled with sea water and bottled beers, plus a group of lads drawing a flaccid penis onto the face of an unconscious victim.

No music was required, given the pirate themed 80s tribute act, Arrr-Ha, had just begun their set and you could hear every word of their first track, 'Aye Aye Wanna Dance with Somebody'.

I couldn't see Alizia amongst the crowd yet but I did make brief eye-contact with Lee, who was grabbing himself a drink from the... bin. He took one look at my t-shirt before smirking to himself.

I decided it was time that I pushed myself out of my comfort-zone to go and strike up a conversation with the guy. It was his party after all.

He took the lead, proclaiming, "It took some balls to put that top back on. I actually respect that."

"Thank you?" I practically asked, amidst my suspicion. Was he being... nice?

"Alizia mentioned she'd invited you along."

"I hope that's okay?"

"I'm used to it," he said. "She has this tendency to latch on to losers that she feels need saving. It's why I made her come off social media. That place is a cesspool of pathetic, needy losers. It wasn't good for her."

The whole 'nice' charade hadn't lasted long. Lee was back in the room. I couldn't help but notice his derogative choice of words. He "*made her*" come off social media - like she was part of his property.

Lee threw me a bottled beer. "Have a drink," he insisted.

I was puzzled that the bottle in my hand, alongside the others floating around in the water, all had their labels torn off them. "Apparently, peeling off the paper is a sign of sexual frustration," I said in a playful manner.

He gave no reaction to my attempt at cracking a joke before explaining seriously, "I get big money from certain drink brands and can't risk being photographed drinking anything that isn't linked to one of my sponsors."

"Well, thank you for the drink offer but I don't do alcohol," I said, attempting to hand back the bottle.

"They're all non-alcoholic beers," he replied. "I don't get drunk around people that I can't trust. I need to be in full control at events like this. Everyone has their cameras ready, hoping you'll take the bait when they give you shit. Of course, the antagonising part never makes it onto the internet. It's always just the aftermath."

Lee began to walk away before turning to conclude, "Help yourself to the drinks. Mingle. Enjoy."

I swallowed a large mouthful of the mysterious drink I'd been handed. The artificial beer flavour alone gave me a sense of guilt - but not quite enough to stop me from drinking it. Besides, I've always felt a little less self-conscious with a drink, or anything, in my hand. It stops me from doing my nervous and highly distracting hand ballet-esque thing, which I do when I'm talking to people I'm not comfortable with. I believe it's more commonly known as 'Jazz Hands'.

The only other people I recognised amongst the crowd were The Taylor Twins. I resolved that I could just about endure the pain of 'small talk' with the duo before Alizia arrived.

With a wave, I was able to grab the attention of Tommy. "Hey," I called out in a larger-than-life and animated voice, mimicking his style for an unbeknownst, subconscious reason.

The entertainer looked at me with disgust. This was an expression I didn't even know he was capable of. "Fuck off, mate," he sneered. "We're off the clock."

An unprofessional response? Yes. But it actually made me like him a little better. It was the one time he actually came across as human.

I fucked off as had been requested and hovered back around the drinks. I must have got through about eight bottles in the forty minutes I spent waiting for Alizia. By the time she finally arrived, I felt quite merry and confident. With no alcohol in the drinks, I whittled it down to the effects of some kind of placebo effect.

Alizia walked past her fiancé to greet me first. This had to bode well for me, right?

"I'm so sorry I'm late," she said.

Unsurprisingly, she looked amazing. In a wonderfully fitted red dress, lit perfectly by the moonlight, she looked like a post-Photoshop catalogue model.

Although I was firmly focused on Alizia, I could still see Lee looking right at me within my peripheral.

"Don't even worry about it," I replied. "I'm just glad you're here now."

"Have I missed much?"

"About nine songs with awful pirate puns, three speeches from Lee and what started as a pretty basic penis drawn onto someone's head now has some detailed veins and ball hair added."

"I'm gutted I missed all that," she joked.

I couldn't wait any longer before asking, "Hey, Alizia, what made you stop doing your social media stuff? I've looked you up. You're great at it."

Whilst opening a bottle for herself, she paused, deep in thought. After taking a moment to consider this, she explained, "I just decided it wasn't for me."

"It wasn't for you or it wasn't for Lee?"

Alizia looked bewildered. Actually, I'd describe it more as insulted. Definitely insulted. If there was a competition to piss someone off in the shortest amount of time with them, I'd be world champion right now.

"One, I make my own choices when it comes to my own life," she snapped. "Two... way to kill the party mood."

Before I had the chance to apologise, Lee had marched his way over. "Babes, when I ask you to be somewhere at 8pm, can you please be there at 8pm," he spoke at her through gritted teeth, snarling.

I jumped in with, "Great way to greet your fiancé!" I know, I know - very hypocritical of me. "Why don't you tell her how beautiful she looks?"

Squaring up to me, Lee increased his aggression. "She knows she looks good. I wouldn't be with her if she didn't look good."

I think there was a compliment for Alizia in there somewhere.

I moved closer to the asshole, standing my ground. Looking him dead in the eyes, I launched my counterattack. "You are a shallow, narcissistic prick who is incapable of loving someone more than you love yourself. Let's see if people are still swooning over you once I've smashed your pretty little face in. You are so lucky to be marrying this woman so give her the respect she deserves."

Alizia moved to stand between the two of us and softly asked me, "What are you doing, Aiden? I think maybe I read you wrong. I feel stupid for thinking that this 'nice guy' facade was for real."

That cut deep. I genuinely believed I was a nice guy. At least, I used to be. I thought about the good things I'd done this past twelve months and, to be honest, they were few and far between.

I felt awful about ruining Alizia's night before it had even begun. I wanted to wipe the slate clean and attempt to explain that this was not my standard way of behaving. I'd never spoken about smashing someone's face in – not once in my entire life. I had no idea how or why those words slipped out. Lee spoke up before I was given the chance to give my apologies. "I'll tell you what he's doing," he said. "Aiden is not handling his booze. A few beers in and he suddenly thinks he's some big man."

Wait. What?

Of course. How could I have been so naive? What I had assumed was a placebo effect or my rising anxiety levels doing funny things to my mind, was, instead, booze kicking in. I had been lied to.

A fresh wave of anger rushed through my veins. Before I knew it, a familiar rage had consumed me.

There was suddenly a contortion of fear across Lee's face. It was the first time I'd seen any other expression from him besides smug.

"Don't touch my face... I'm a model," he pleaded.

It wasn't enough to stop me pouncing on top of him, pushing and pulling us both onto the ground. With absolutely no hesitation, I had punched him across his left cheek, then the right and back to the other - each punch more powerful than the last.

I had most definitely lost control.

I worry whether I'd have stopped at all had it not have been for several people pulling me away from him.

A voice in my head jeered, "*Way to show Alizia you're a nice guy.*"

I watched on stunned and horrified as Lee covered his bloody face with his hands. His fiance was comforting him whilst staring at me with a look of both shock and disappointment. It was a look I had grown accustomed to, but she was the last person I wanted to see it from. It was then that the gravity of the situation really hit me.

"You need to leave," Alizia said calmly but firmly.

I desperately tried to think of something to say to rectify the situation but my mind was blank. I admitted defeat and reluctantly began to walk away.

I'd only made it a few steps when out of nowhere, I could see Tracey running towards me. I'd never been so happy to see her. Finally, one person here that could perhaps see the situation from my point of view. Imagine my disappointment when my own sister rushed straight past me and instead towards her idol. Once upon a time, it was me on that pedestal. That changed exactly one year ago. Everything changed one year ago and it had become increasingly apparent that things were never going to get better.

Feeling numb, I continued to stumble away from the carnage.

As the sounds of Lee's panicked cries about his modelling career became more faint, the sounds of Arrr-Ha grew louder. This time they were ruining an Otis Redding classic with 'Sitting on the Deck of the Ship'.

This is certainly not how I'd imagined the evening unfolding. Sure, I envisioned saying or doing something wrong, but not on such a spectacular scale.

I needed to pass out on my bed. I desperately wanted for this horrific day to be over.

During the short journey between the beach and the family caravan, the booze had taken even more of an effect on me. I was so drunk that I almost stumbled straight into the swimming pool. Shortly after, I was so certain I'd seen my mum's friend, Karen, I almost called out to her. I was a mess.

Once I had staggered my way over in the direction of the poolside bar, there was one thing unfolding before me that I knew I was not imagining. My mum was openly and ignorantly kissing the barman she had been flirting with at the welcome event earlier in the day.

The rage was back.

I wanted to storm over towards them and plead for her to just once, consider the rest of the family and to remind her how we needed her now, more than ever.

What would have been the point though? This wouldn't have been new information to her.

I was done arguing. I was done hurting. Every day was a new battle and I had no more fight left within me.

I turned to look at the tall tower of flats in the distance - the one that resembled the building in my dreams. You could barely see it in the dark of the night, but there it was - the key to what I was now convinced, was my one and only escape from my own suffering – and everyone else's.

Could I actually go through with it though? Actually, yes, I truly believed that I could.

There was only one thing I could think of in that moment that might have been able to stop me. I fantasised that mum would have a sudden burst of clarity before pushing the barman away from her. In this fantasy, she'd turn to me and explain how she was sorry and that everything was going to be better from this point on. I really do believe that this would have been enough for me to shake away the dark thoughts consuming me.

Within this reality though, she continued playing tonsil tennis with the sleaze, that I'd no doubts, had played that very game with numerous other women that week alone.

My decision was made.

I headed towards the tall silhouette that loomed over me. This darkened building would put an end to the hurt, once and for all. With one leap, this living nightmare would finally be over.

Chapter Seven: The Day Before Happys - Tracey's Story

For better or for worse, a person's life can dramatically change in a single moment. It just takes one chance encounter with a complete stranger, one email or telephone call and like that, things will never be the same again.

I was both excited and terrified at the thought of potentially having one of those moments within the next hour.

I sat in an empty maths room, taking deep breaths to try and calm my nerves.

Most students were currently rushing home now that the final bell had rung, signalling the end of the school day. Not me. I was waiting anxiously for Abi Brewer to walk through the classroom door.

She was by far the most popular girl and biggest social media influencer at our school. Rumour has it, she hasn't had to pay for a Nandos for almost two years. Why? Because one single post of Abi Brewer taking a selfie beside a plate of Peri Peri Chicken was enough to fill that restaurant with entirely new customers for months afterwards.

Each student at our school worshipped Abi Brewer and in contrast, every teacher feared her. Ever since she referred to Mrs Forty as "Mrs Farty" in one of her hate videos, that nickname is all anyone now uses - including the head teacher. Fart machines are regularly heard going off as many as one-hundred times throughout each of her classes – which do at least drown out the awkward sounds of her crying.

The local legend recently announced that she was creating a new group of social influencers. The idea is that once each member was done with school, the entire group would house share in some multi-media functioning, six-bedroom mansion where those living within it would eat and sleep video content. It sounded like heaven.

Abi Brewer had somehow heard about my YouTube channel and even more unbelievably, she'd invited me along to interview for the position of the sixth and final member of the group.

When Abi Brewer finally marched through the door, I was breathless. She was like a Goddess and she was here, right now, to talk to me. Me!

Elegantly, she glided her way across the room towards me. Abi Brewer's face changed from warm and inviting to disappointed - perhaps even disgusted.

I hadn't so much as uttered a single word yet, so I had to assume my look just wasn't good enough.

I tried not to overthink something that was likely fabricated in my own head - a terrible habit of mine. Besides, I didn't need to add more pressure to the stress I was already feeling.

"Let's do this quick. I'm already bored," Abi Brewer sniped, whilst pulling up a chair opposite me. She took a small notepad and pen from her pocket before firing questions at me. "Tell me why you deserve my sixth and final position."

"Well," I replied sheepish. "I do it all. I film and edit all my videos myself. I'm getting much better in front of a camera and I know with your guidance, I can excel even further. I'll do whatever you say. I want this more than anything. I've even been saving all year to upgrade my camera.

I have almost seven-hundred pounds."

My heart sunk as I watched Abi Brewer openly write down the words 'Too desperate'.

"Seven-hundred pounds? Cute. I received more than that this morning for taking a sip of some crappy energy drink," she said pretentiously. "The successful applicant will ideally have at least one hundred thousand subscribers. You left that part of the form blank - so what kind of number are we looking at?"

My heart sank further still as I mumbled, "...Two."

Abi Brewer livened up a little. "Two hundred thousand? Not bad," she almost cheered.

"No. Two. Just two."

"...Right. Let me tell you about the rest of the team. First, there's me... Abi Brewer. I know the game better than anyone you're likely to ever meet. Lara is our fashion and makeup guru. Brandy specialises in fitness. Cara's daddy is really rich and Leanne is happy to display an epic cleavage. What is it that you would bring to the table?"

"Literally, anything you want."

Abi Brewer circled the words 'Too desperate', which much confirmed it was game over for me. I wasn't good enough.

"Look, it's never going to happen to you," she declared. "I can just tell that you don't have it. You'll always just be that girl who is related to... Mummy's Little Princess."

Although not surprised, I was still gutted to hear these words spoken out loud, confirming my insecurities were totally valid.

I knew this would be my last chance to speak to the girl who had always blanked me before now and would continue to do so as soon as she left the room. As Abi Brewer began to leave, I shouted, "With respect, I'll prove you all wrong! The biggest content creators out there all had just two subscribers once upon a time. I'll get there. Maybe I can get there a little quicker with some advice?"

"Fine," she responded reluctantly. "Let me guess... most of your videos, if not all, are about you. Story times. Your feelings. Shit like that?"

"...Yes," I sighed, feeling exposed and vulnerable.

"I assumed so. Your subscriber numbers confirm that nobody gives a shit about you. Create content that entertains or educates. Anything that offers some kind of value. Review something, prank somebody for laughs, give a homeless person a sandwich. Do anything but talk about yourself."

These words were a particularly hard pill to swallow. Sure, Abi Brewer could have been a little bit more sensitive with her choice of words, but I guess it made sense. I didn't get the chance to say thank you for her time. She was gone.

I took a longer route on my walk home that evening so I could digest and properly reflect on the advice I'd so bluntly been given.

I felt so stupid I'd wasted such a huge amount of time on creating content that nobody would ever see, or care about, if they were to ever miraculously stumble upon it. With this being said, I did also feel optimistic about moving forward. The one girl at our school that knew just what she was talking about when it came to succeeding on social media had given me a new direction to head towards. I was so grateful to her for that. I knew how lucky I was.

By taking the lengthy, alternative route home, I just so happened to cross paths with a homeless man. Abi Brewer had mentioned making content about the homeless minutes prior to this. Perhaps this was fate?

If I'd have had my camera with me to capture the moment, I'd have stopped to give a donation, or something to eat – hell, maybe even a hotel room for the evening to sleep in with some of the cash I'd saved – hopefully making it back off of the video revenue. Next time.

For now, another video content idea hit me. Abi Brewer had also mentioned prank videos being popular and I giggled to myself, confident I had a great one in mind.

I had previously been pissed off that Aiden was asked to attend our weekly family counselling session alone - like he was the golden child and his feelings mattered more than my own. Maybe that decision was fate too? Usually my brother never left his room but for once he was away for a good hour or so. This would be just long enough to put my plan into action.

Dad was quite the hoarder and as a result, we had about fifty unfolded cardboard boxes in our garage for if and when we should need them. Now was that time.

It took me a good forty minutes to drag my brother's bed and couch into my room. In their place, I used the boxes and sheets to give the illusion that his furniture had not been tampered with. Returning home, Aiden would inevitably rush to his room and dive on his bed - instead, crashing through the boxes. Of course, I would be there with my camera in hand and just like that... comedy gold.

My idea was influenced by another video I'd seen recently. Lee Lauren had created a huge, 8ft deep hole in his parents living room - covering it with a rug. Watching his mother fall through it in slow motion was hilarious.

Like an absolute sweetheart, Lee Lauren bought a brand new car for his mother to make up for the broken arm she ended up with as a result of the prank.

Once everything was set up for the big moment, I impatiently waited in my bedroom, desperate to hear the sweet sound of our front door opening. I used this time to fantasise that uploading this prank would be the defining moment that would change everything. Maybe, just maybe this video would be the one that finally raked in the views and then I would be the one getting all the male attention at school. I would be the one getting free chicken. Abi Brewer and her gang would practically be begging me to join their club.

When the front door finally crashed open, my spirits were elevated further. I was so giddy.

As predicted, Aiden wasted no time in rushing up to his room.

Excitedly, I grabbed my camera. It was show time.

I crept through the hallway, desperately trying to avoid areas I knew would creek and therefore potentially blow my cover.

Fortunately, Aiden had left his door ajar.

I hit record on the camera, meaning I would be ready for the money shot that would be any moment now.

My brother grabbed his guitar from the wall, which, to be honest, made me slightly nervous. That instrument meant a lot to him and if this prank was in any way responsible for it breaking - well, I'd never hear the end of it.

I ultimately decided to take the chance and persist with the plan.

With guitar in hand, he went to fall backwards onto what he thought was his bed. Success. I was ecstatic.

I was able to capture the moment before turning the camera towards myself and declaring, "To the haters that thought my brother wouldn't be stupid enough to fall for this prank, you were wrong. To all those in Team Tracey that knew I'd pull it off... love to you!"

My excitement was cut short once I saw the expression on my brothers face. He looked pissed. I mean, he always looked stressed but this was different. Not once had I ever seen him looking this mad.

"I'm sorry. It was just a joke," I said defensively.

He charged at me and I genuinely feared for my own wellbeing. Not once had I felt that way around my brother. All I could do in that moment was cower with my arm reached out in a desperate attempt to protect myself.

Nobody had ever left me this scared. The fact that my own brother was the perpetrator made it all the more heart-breaking.

I was embarrassed that I'd allowed him to see me so vulnerable.

"I'm done playing your games!" He screamed.

"I know... I know. I'm sorry," I pleaded as calmly as possible, desperate to get my annoying but kind brother back.

I tried to take some comfort in the thought that if he was going to hurt me, it probably would have happened by now - but this was all still unfamiliar territory so anything could have happened.

"Play your stupid games with your stupid friends all you like," he snarled. "Just keep me out of it!"

"I can't upload a video for the next three days so I wanted to make this particular one a gooden."

"You can't upload for three whole days? How awful," continued the verbal abuse. "Who cares? You have two subscribers and one of them is me. I can therefore confirm that at least half of your following does not give a shit about you!"

My brother may not have hurt me physically but those words cut me to my core. To make it worse, it was the second time I'd heard the comment today alone.

At risk of hearing anything else that simply couldn't be taken back, I dashed towards my own room. The moment I was within my own safe space; I broke down in tears.

Collapsed onto my bed, I tried to process everything that had just happened - to try and see things from his perspective - but I couldn't do it. There was absolutely no excuse for his behaviour.

I hadn't been thinking for very long when I heard Uncle Dave swearing from inside the kitchen. This meant dinner was just around the corner but I wasn't hungry. Even if I had been there was no way I was going to leave this room and risk having to see Aiden again. I just wanted to be alone.

Actually, no, there was one person I craved to see and right on cue, he entered the room.

Dad always knew when I needed him the most. It's like my broken heart projects a spotlight into the night sky and he's my real life Batman.

"About your brother," Dad said gently whilst sitting beside me on the bed. "It's not a great time for him. Of course, it's not a great time for any of us - but Aiden blames himself for what happened. He thinks we blame him too and that's a lot to deal with. The more you believe that people see you as the villain, the easier it is to play the part. But he'll get there. I know he's devastated about his actions just now."

I had nothing to say in reply and as always, Dad knew that. He hugged me before leaving me to my thoughts.

I was supposed to be spending an entire weekend with Aiden. I couldn't think of anything worse now that this had happened. I knew regardless of whatever my brother had to say or do, I would never, ever, within my lifetime, forgive him.

Chapter Eight: The Audition - Tracey's Story

It took approximately seven hours to forgive Aiden.

It's amazing what a good night's sleep can do. I was still annoyed, hurt and upset about what had happened, sure, but it meant a lot more to me that I at least try and help make our weekend away work for the entire family. That meant making a conscious effort to draw a line and move on.

It seemed that my brother had also wiped the slate clean and was making an effort himself. He had made everyone breakfast ahead of venturing to Happys - all our favourite foods placed in individually labelled brown paper bags. One by one, each family member grabbed their own pack up before taking it to their own preferred area of the house to eat it. I forget the last time we'd all had a meal together as a family.

Another kind gesture came courtesy of my brother wearing his 'Mummy's Little Princess' t-shirt. He knew it would raise a smile on our mother's face and it did just that.

Tucking into my crisp sandwich breakfast, I took pleasure in thinking about the days ahead. I was excited by the thought of a change of scenery. I had a friend recently ask if the holiday would bring up too many painful memories of previous years, when he would have been there with us. I simply replied that it made no difference. He was in my thoughts all day, every day - so why would it matter where we were?

My excitement towards our holiday catapulted to epic heights once I saw who else would be there at the same time as us. Flicking through my phone on the train, my hands shook as I read that the one and only Lee Lauren would be on-site to film an advert. I squealed with delight. He was literally my favourite YouTuber and just like that, there was an actual chance I might get to see him in the flesh!

I felt a sense that the universe must be guiding me to greater things ever since my conversation with Abi Brewer. This was further proof.

If you needed even more evidence that some kind of supernatural force was at play here, it was like my brother had been possessed... this time in a good way. Basically, Lee Lauren had posted that he was judging a talent show on-site and unbelievably, Aiden agreed to attend the auditions - potentially giving me the opportunity to speak to my hero. My brother even went as far as agreeing to audition himself, to further increase any chance of a meet and greet. This was totally out of character for him. It had been so long since he had performed publicly and he was doing so as a favour to me. For whatever reason, something felt positively different. Rather than question it, I chose to ride that wave.

In the entertainment hall, I was sat so close to Lee Lauren, I could smell his cologne. He smelt incredible and looked even better. I was able to divert my eyes away from this beautiful specimen for around one minute - practically the duration of my brother singing a song he had written years ago. During those sixty seconds, Aiden looked happy - more so than I'd seen in a long time. I liked seeing him this way again and so, in turn, I felt content for the first time in ages and I found myself sharing in his happy energy. That may be hard to believe from someone that usually took great pleasure in winding him up, but honestly, seeing my brother up there so content and merry filled me with joy.

As the song came to an end, the audience erupted with applause. I could not have been prouder and I could see how much this moment meant to Aiden. I was also quite relieved on my own behalf; given that I had been the one to put my brother in this situation.

These positive vibes were short lived, sadly. Lee Lauren stated on the mic for all to hear that Aiden was insensitive to have sung a song about sugary treats – given that he was diabetic.

I felt awful for Aiden being up there, vulnerable, with all eyes on him. I was proud once more, when bravely, he stood his ground and ultimately, his act made it through to the next days' final performance.

I feared his back and forth with Lee Lauren was going to be enough to put Aiden back in a foul mood. Incredibly, it did not. *Phew.*

The internet star had announced for all of those who had made it through to perform the following day, to see him to get further information so they could prepare for the talent show. Meanwhile, I was preparing for Aiden to demand we leave immediately, but this new and encouraging version of himself suggested that I go in his place.

I was petrified and entirely unprepared mentally. This was a scenario I had dreamt and often fantasised about but I never actually envisioned it happening for real. *Oh my God, oh my God...*

The closer in the queue I got to Lee Lauren, the more I began to hyperventilate. By the time just one person was between him and I, I could barely breath at all.

I could hear Lee Lauren praising the young boy that went by the name Lil Problemz. "Seriously, you've got talent," he said sweetly. "You got any other rhymes you can spit out?"

"Yeah, loads," the boy beamed.

"Well, let's hear some."

Lil Problemz took a moment to gather his thoughts before rapping,

"Clean your plate. Take out the bin.
What am I, your slave?
Is this my life now, huh? No wonder I misbehave.
Darren gets to stay up till ten, I go to bed at nine.
He gets Pepsi with his dinner, I get water at mine.
You can do better, ma. Be like Darren's mum.
I'll get her on the phone to tell you how it's done."

"I love it," Lee Lauren encouraged. "Mums, aye? I totally get it. Mine used to force me to eat my vegetables. Not anymore. Ironically, I paid her ten grand recently to eat ten onions in a row like they were apples."

"I saw that video. Classic."

"I was worried there wasn't enough footage to make it past the standard ten-minute mark after we'd cut out all the demonetising vomiting, but we got there. Ten minutes and fourteen seconds. Cha Ching!"

The internet star proudly patted the young boy on the shoulders before concluding. "You're going to be performing about mid-way through the show tomorrow - right after some crappy astronaut impressionist. I'll be honest, there's a lot of shit acts prior to your performance, so I'm going to need you to bring your A-game. Reel 'em back in."

"I will," Lil Problemz promised before boldly skipping away.

I was next. *Shit*.

Lee Lauren looked towards me in a puzzled manner. "I don't recall you Auditioning?"

"I doo doo," I stuttered nervously. Humiliated, I scrambled to correct myself. "I didn't... is what I meant to say!"

I could feel my cheeks glowing red with unadulterated embarrassment.

"It's okay, I get it," he reassured me. "I am the 'Titty Guy' after all."

"I'm here on Aiden's behalf," I said whilst twiddling my fingers, feeling timid and insecure in front of such a big star.

Lee Lauren looked over towards my brother. He looked annoyed that Aiden was chatting away to his fiancé.

"Tell him that he'll be going up on stage after Lil Problemz," he snapped in a serious tone that confirmed to me that he was indeed bothered by the conversation across the room. "Who are you, anyway? His girlfriend?"

"I'm his sister."

I could tell he was desperately trying not to keep peeking over in their direction but he couldn't help himself.

"It's a shame you didn't audition instead of him. You're way cuter," he said before laughing in an excessively exaggerated manner.

I stood, confused. Was the joke that I actually wasn't cute?

I caught Lee Lauren paying another subtle glance towards Aiden and Alizia and it dawned on me that he was actually trying to make them jealous.

I gave out an awkward laugh too - feeling an obligation to follow suit.

"So, you don't sing? Dance?" he sighed, frustrated that he had not been able to attract his partner's attention away from Aiden.

"No. I am a content creator though... like you."

"You have twelve million subscribers and a mansion?"

"No."

"Then you're not a content creator like me. But you could be."

I quickly perked up. "What do you mean?"

"Well, you could attend one of my training seminars."

My heart once again fell to its familiar, sunken position. I'd seen how expensive these seminars were - tens of thousands of pounds to attend. "They're a little out of my budget," I replied.

"How much have you got?"

"I've saved up seven-hundred, but that's for new equipment."

"That'll do."

"What will do? I'm confused."

"The equipment can wait. That stuff will always be there. I, however, will not. Transfer me the seven-hundred and in return, I'll let you follow me around whilst I shoot this advert. Between scenes, I'll tell you everything you need to know to make it big on YouTube."

I jumped at the offer, snapping up the opportunity before he changed his mind. "Yup, okay!" I squealed in delight. *Yes!*

I'd always clung on to that hope that life can change for the better in just one single moment.

This was most definitely my moment.

Chapter Nine: "What can you do for me?" - Tracey's Story

They say you can't polish a turd but you can cover it in glitter. This is what the staff had tried to do with Lee Lauren's own private caravan. With a small red carpet outside leading to the doorway and crystal lamps, refreshments and official Lee Lauren merchandise filling the interior - they wanted their guest to feel welcome and special.

Taking a break between shooting scenes for the advert, it was just him and I relaxing inside.

I sat on the small couch whilst trying to discreetly wipe my clammy hands on my jeans, so Lee Lauren wouldn't notice how nervous I was.

Having just filmed himself diving off 'The Dynamite Board', he was topless and my God, he looked like he'd never so much as touched a carb in his entire life.

I was caught off guard when he sat right beside me - still topless, might I add. He was close enough to me that his arm hairs were brushing against my own. It gave me goosebumps.

I'd have loved to play it cool, of course, but I didn't know how long this moment would last and I desperately wanted proof that it actually happened. "Can I get a selfie?" I hoped my request hadn't sounded as pathetic as it felt.

"Yes. But not now," he snapped without hesitation. "I've learnt the hard way not to take pictures with people in situations that could easily be misconstrued."

"Okay," I whispered. I was disheartened knowing that without photographic evidence, nobody would ever believe me that I was sat alone with Lee Lauren, who just so happened to be half naked.

"Let's talk about your YouTube channel," he said, steering the interaction away from my request.

Just as I was about to respond, a knock came at the door. Lee Lauren dramatically leapt a few spaces away from me before calling out, "Yes, what?"

Tammy Taylor entered the caravan, looking particularly nervous. "Slight problem with the next scene," she said timidly - a far cry from her usual energetic demeanour.

"Go on," Lee Lauren snapped at Tammy, unimpressed.

"I know you really wanted to release a bunch of balloons, but we simply can't do that. Not here anyway. Not with the nature reserve right round the corner."

"And why not?"

Tammy started to fidget and stammered, "Well... it's just the animals may eat the rubber and then... well, they could die."

"Release the balloons and then apologise to whoever afterwards. Plead ignorance. Pay a fine if you have to!"

"I... I just thought that maybe the scene wasn't worth... animals dying. I watched all five videos on you being a vegan so I thought that-"

"You thought wrong! Get the scene ready and I'll be out there once it is. Stop wasting my time with shit excuses to do half a job." The aggression in his voice reverberated through me and I looked over at Tammy. She gave a forced smile but I could see her lips struggle as they quivered. With a nod, she backed away and leaving, closed the door again behind her.

Lee Lauren wasted no time in sliding back beside me, this time skin touching skin. "The staff here are incompetent," he said. "They're just awful."

I replied. "There's one staff member I really liked. Jenny Happy. She's the young daughter of the owner. Not sure if she still works-"

"She doesn't. Thank God!" He didn't let me finish my sentence before cutting me off. It seemed the mere mention of her name had struck a nerve.

"You know her?"

"Unfortunately, yes. She's fucking crazy."

"She seemed lovely to me."

"Well, she's not," he snarled before shaking off his negative energy. "Sorry," he said much calmer. "You're probably thinking I'm some terrible person with the whole balloon thing."

I sat in awkward silence before Lee Lauren continued, "I just care about this advert. If I put my name to something, I want whatever it is to be as good as it can be - even if that makes me look like the bad guy."

He let out a defeated sigh before continuing, "I'm always the villain. As a prime example, I'm guessing you saw the leaked footage of me changing my mind about giving some homeless guy that twenty grand?"

"Erm... I think that vaguely rings a bell," I lied. I knew exactly what he was talking about. The media got hold of footage showing Lee Lauren giving a large sum of money placed in a suitcase to a man that had been sleeping rough in the streets. When the homeless man barely reacted to the gesture, he was ordered to give it all back due to the lack of tears he had shed - resulting in, as Lee Lauren put it, "Shit footage."

"Everyone talks about that day," the celebrity said softly. "But do you know what nobody talks about? The follow up video. I paid for that homeless guy to take acting lessons so I could redo the video a month later and get an actual performance out of him. He was media ready and he eventually got his money. But nobody cares about that part of the story."

"Sure. Right," I responded awkwardly. I was becoming increasingly anxious that Lee Lauren might get called away any minute now and that I might miss out on the valuable advice I'd paid a whopping seven-hundred pounds to get. "Do you mind if we talk about my channel now?"

Lee Lauren stared at me insulted. I was relieved to see his mood lighten again as his face softened a few moments later. His emotions seemed to be all over the place. He grinned and spoke again, "You're quite bossy, aren't you? I like it. It's sexy."

I let myself down as the all-too-familiar squeal found its way out of me. How could I have remained composed after hearing those words coming from this absolute God?

"What's your channel called?" he asked.

Still blushing from the compliment, I replied, "Another Bloody YouTuber."

"I hate it."

Oh. The flattery was short lived.

I was disheartened hearing those words but I tried to push my ego to one side and keep an open mind. After all, my channel was, and always had been, dead and his was thriving. So, I waited with baited breath for his wisdom to help me get to where he was.

Lee Lauren continued, "Your channel name isn't personal enough. People are more likely to invest in a person rather than what sounds like a brand. The best piece of advice I can give you is..."

He paused, leaving me on tenterhooks.

"You know what, I'll be honest with you. I could tell you how to improve your content, sure. But that will only get you so far. It's not what you know, it's who you know. If some huge content creator hadn't reposted my titty video, there's no way I'd be where I am today. I will always be grateful to him for that. I could mention you in one of my videos and your channel will explode within seconds. And I might just do that."

As his tease hung in mid-air, he placed his hand firmly on my thigh before leaning in to almost whisper, "You know, I don't usually give advice out like this. Essentially, you'd become my competitor, but you're different. There's something I like about you. I think you can help me out too." I could feel his breath on my neck.

My heart began to race - though I could no longer compute whether it was doing so through excitement, or in fear.

This was not how I had imagined this situation unfolding.

Lee Lauren's free hand moved across my shoulder, his rough fingers grazing against my skin. His arm, now wrapping around my shoulder, felt restrictive. His hand explored further still, until it was on my breast. Gradually, he tightened his grip around it.

My heart was in my throat. I was frozen, completely unable to move. All I could do was sit here, as if I was Medusa's latest victim. Or was this a blessing? I was so confused.

My father had warned me numerous times to get myself out of situations like this. Scream, run and fight back - whatever it took.

This was so different though. Lee Lauren was nothing like those old, obese predators that had featured in the tedious 'life-lesson' videos we were made to watch at school. He wasn't the weirdo lurking in the alley that Dad had warned me to avoid. This was my idol. I'd admittedly fantasised about him wanting me in this way many, many times.

I could be close to becoming a successful YouTuber and my actual celebrity crush was attracted to me. How could this be a bad thing?

It just didn't feel right. I could visualise Dad looking at me, heartbreak on his face. My subconscious was answering my own internal question. This was wrong.

As Lee Lauren leant in for a kiss I was able to force a croak, "No, I can't. I'm sorry."

This didn't seem to deter him from continuing. If anything, it felt like his hands were gripping tighter as he said, "Sex with a celebrity is still just sex. Relax."

Sex? I didn't even want to kiss him; let alone did I want to sleep with him!

The hand that was still on my thigh started to move slowly towards my crotch. He continued, "You're special. All the girls who want me would be so jealous of you now. It feels good, doesn't it - that I'm choosing you?"

It took every ounce of courage within me to shout, "Stop!"

"Why?" he screamed.

He sounded angry but looked more confused. I sensed that he hadn't been rejected in quite some time.

Embarrassed and humiliated, I muttered, "I'm fifteen."

He released his hold on me, pushing me backwards into the back of the couch. "You didn't think to tell me this sooner?" he asked furiously.

Dad had also spoken to me many times about manipulation and victim blaming. It's interesting how words of wisdom can often be perceived as whining and over worrying, right up until you find yourself in the very situations you'd been warned of. My father would have been proud to hear me ask, "You didn't think to ask me how old I was? And why should it have even mattered when I'm purely here to talk about my channel?"

"Why the fuck would I want to talk about your shitty little YouTube channel?"

Lee had now lost the ability to hurt me with his words. My embarrassment shifted and I now felt absolutely furious. I felt the rage from the very tips of my toes, rising within me. I wasn't just angry - l was irreparably disappointed in him. I was no longer looking at him on the pedestal I had once placed him upon.

Lee took a deep breath in an attempt to control his own anger before continuing through a forced smile, "I'm totally kidding. You'll come across this type of behaviour a lot in this industry and you handled it like a pro. You passed the test."

I was young but I wasn't stupid. I could see through his attempt to gaslight me. I could smell the desperation.

There were so many things that I wanted to say to Lee and perhaps I should have. However, it felt imperative that I get myself out of this situation and so, I moved to the door and left.

Once I was out of the caravan, I felt instantly safer and back in control. This contrast helped me realise that I had indeed just endured a traumatic experience. Lee called out in one final defeated plea, "Come back. I was testing you."

I ignored him and continued to walk, picking up my pace. With each step I took away from him and the further away I got, the lighter and stronger I became.

Sat in my caravan bedroom, I could hear Aiden in the room next door. He was watching Alizia's videos. I recognised her voice instantly. I wanted to knock on his door and share the news of my new hatred towards the guy that he clearly detested also. I think I wanted to feel protected for a while too. Sadly, we didn't really have that kind of relationship anymore, so I left him be.

Instead, I used my phone to flick through Lee's video thumbnails. I felt like I was seeing him through fresh eyes - ones that saw right through all of his bullshit. Then self-doubt crept in and I wondered if I'd overreacted. *Was it just a test?* He said I was special. *Did he mean that?* I felt a stabbing pain in my breast, where he'd grabbed it so tightly and my doubt again vanished. I fucking hated him for making me feel this way.

The homeless guy in Lee's video… his friends… me… even his own mother - we all had something in common. We were all pawns in a game that had just one winner... Lee Lauren.

It dawned on me that I was actually aspiring to be like this. No wonder my brother barely wanted to be around me anymore.

I was haunted by the memory of passing by the homeless man just one day prior. I gave him nothing, simply because I wasn't able to document the moment. I didn't see him as a human being. I'm ashamed to say that I actually saw him as nothing more than viewing numbers. I felt overwhelmingly ashamed and consumed with guilt.

I needed a distraction.

I instinctively turned to YouTube for my dose of escapism, but this time I had no interest in watching the channels I'd usually have gone to. It turns out there was much more to the website than Lee Lauren causing his mum distress in the name of "comedy" or Abi Brewer flexing her freebies.

I discovered some smaller channels. Real, humble people just being themselves. No gimmicks.

A quick search revealed that there were others that had been through similar situations to the one I had just found myself in with Lee. Victims that felt pressured into doing things that they didn't want to do. In their videos, they were honestly and openly discussing the manipulation and how they'd overcome the painful aftermath. Their video numbers were low but that didn't devalue their message. Before today, I may have shamefully thought that it did.

How could I have been so naive?

I responded to the couple of videos that I had watched to express the admiration I felt towards the creators and how I had heard - and more importantly, believed every word that they had to say.

I wondered just how many people out there were suffering in silence. How many people had Lee treated like a commodity, to be used and thrown out at his whim?

I began to cry. These were not just tears brought on through my own self-pity. Many came as a result of feeling tremendous empathy towards the other victims out there. Victims that didn't have the strength to persist within the rules that no couldn't ever translate to mean anything else, but no.

I must have lay in bed sobbing for around five minutes, when I heard my brother leaving his room. I prepared myself for the inevitable interrogation, surrounding my well-being. I'd no doubt that he would have heard my cries, especially given just how paper-thin these caravan walls were.

Seeing Aiden's shadow stop beneath my door, I began to panic. I had no idea how honest I wanted to be just yet. Even if I were to tell him everything, he'd probably just say how it was my own fault for getting myself in that situation. I knew I couldn't hear that yet because a fragment of me believed it myself. I needed to process it all for a bit longer.

I concluded that once he'd asked what was wrong with me, I'd simply explain how I'd tell him everything once I was comfortable to do so.

Here's the thing... despite knowing I was so upset; the knock never came. No words of encouragement through the door. Nothing. My brother chose to just leave me in this state and I won't lie... that really hurt.

It was my Uncle that came to my aid. "Can I come in?" he asked sheepish.

"I guess."

Uncle Dave cautiously opened the door. He had a look about him that screamed to me that he was uncomfortable being in this situation. He softly queried, "What are you doing?"

"Watching YouTube."

"Are you sad because your videos aren't very good?"

"No," I snapped, offended.

"Are you sad because of... woman trouble stuff?"

"Sure," I lied, desperate for this interaction to be over.

Looking even more unsure whether he should be having this chat, Uncle Dave continued, "Sometimes... a girl's body does scary things. It can... be confusing. One could describe it as the elevator door scene in The Shinning and-"

"Red card!"

"Yeah, that's probably for the best," he said. Uncle Dave took a moment before adding, "Listen... I was kind of hoping you were going to be out around now. I just really fancied some time alone."

"Well, I was really hoping to just relax in bed. Maybe watch a few more videos."

"You can't live your life through a screen. When I was your age, I had the best time playing a whole bunch of different games with my friends. None of which, involved electronics."

"What kind of games?"

"Well," he replied in deep thought. "For starters, there was 'stick hit'."

"What's that?"

"My friends and I would hit each other with sticks."

"Anything else?"

"We would also play... 'shit stick'."

"And that is?"

"My friends and I would hit each other with sticks... with shit on them."

Uncle Dave could see that his attempt to paint a picture of 'better times' was failing, miserably. In one final, desperate plea to get me gone, he continued, "Look, just trust me… you don't want to be here in this caravan for the next hour and a half."

"Consider me gone," I said without hesitation, genuinely terrified as to what lie ahead within these walls.

In that moment I decided that if I could push myself to leave this caravan, I was going to push myself even further. Lee was going to hear what I had to say to him.

With that, I wasted no more time before marching out of the caravan. I'd heard rumours of a beach party that he'd be attending and so headed straight in that direction – well, after a lot of pacing back and forth throughout the Happys resort, attempting to build up my courage. Once I eventually reached the destination, lo and behold, that's where I found my target.

To get to Lee, I had to march past my brother.

At the time, it hadn't even occurred to me that it was odd seeing Aiden there. My mind was solely focused on my imminent speech.

When I'd finally reached the perpetrator, I was taken aback. Laying on the sand, it was clear to me that he'd just been involved in some kind of a fight. His hands were covering his bloody face. He was a mess.

Old habits and well practiced manners, made me want to apologise for catching Lee at such a bad time and that I'd return when it was more convenient. That would have been the easy way out though - something I'd grown accustomed to but wanted to change.

I stood my ground. I visualised the victims in the videos I'd just watched. I imagined them standing beside Lee, encouraging me to face my aggressor and giving him some home truths in person - a luxury they had been deprived of.

"Lee," I shouted, desperately trying to be heard above all the commotion.

He looked directly at me before sniping, "Clearly this is not a good time. Piss off!"

Again, I almost left with my tail between my legs. But, no. He was going to hear what I had to tell him. Right here. Right now. "No. I will most certainly not just piss off. You will listen to what someone else has to say for a change!"

The background noise became quieter. People had become intrigued by the situation that was unfolding before them.

Alizia approached me in a composed manner. "What's this all about?"

"I'll tell you," Lee shouted, scrambling for justification. "She's crazy! Just like her brother. She's probably drunk too!"

Alizia looked at me, concerned. I think she could see how important it was for me to speak up before I lost my courage. "Say it," she told me before telling Lee, "You'll listen to what she has to say."

I took a deep breath. "I know you don't even know my name," I said, trying desperately to not let him see me getting so emotionally upset. "You saw me as an easy pay cheque and then you saw me as an easy fuck - but you were wrong. My name is Tracey Gardener. I'm a daughter. I'm a sister. I'm a human being and not some toy for you to throw away when you're finished playing with it."

Lee laughed. "See... bat shit crazy," he pleaded with Alizia, who didn't respond. I could see she was gracefully trying to process it all.

Standing up for myself more than ever before was possibly the most difficult thing I'd done, but having done so, I now had absolute clarity. With a sudden clearer frame of mind, the realisation dawned on me that Lee had implied my brother had been drinking alcohol. That can't have been true. There's no way he'd have touched a drop of booze - not after what happened last year. Something wasn't right.

Call it sibling intuition, but I somehow knew that if I were to look up at the dark silhouette of the nearby block of flats, I'd see the outline of Aiden standing above it. I took a deep breath to compose myself before looking in that direction and just as I had feared, there he was.

"Fuck," I shouted before sprinting off for help.

I was overcome with regret that the strong bond my brother and I had once had, had deteriorated over the last year. Before then, I'd have known exactly what to say to calm Aiden down, even in the most extreme of situations. Now though, whatever I said just seemed to worsen his mood.

I ran as fast as my legs could move in the direction of the family caravan, knowing Uncle Dave was having his mysterious night in, doing... actually, I didn't want to think about what he could of been doing. He wouldn't usually have been my first choice for support but he was the only person in the family whose whereabouts I was certain of at the time.

  Along the way back towards our caravan was an outdoor bar, where I saw mum snogging the barman she'd been flirting with earlier in the day. It was a disappointing sight but it was obviously not my biggest concern currently.

  "Mum," I shouted breathlessly.

  She looked at me with an overwhelming sense of shame and fear - like I was the authoritative figure in this relationship. "I... explain," mum pleaded whilst slurring her words. "He... a man. Me... a woman."

  Still attached to Mum, the barman remained silent - looking awkwardly in pretty much every other direction but towards me.

  It was painfully obvious Mum was drunk. Looking at her dilated pupils, I feared it wasn't just alcohol she'd had this evening.

  "We need to get Uncle Dave, right now" I pleaded.

  "What... wrong?" Her face dropped. It would seem she was at least sober enough to pick up on the serious tone of my plea.

  "It's Aiden," I sobbed, tears now rushing down my cheeks. I looked up towards the flats where he remained. "It's him. I know it. I think he's going to jump!"

  The slimy prick my mum had been kissing grabbed his coat. He got up and explained, "Hearing you whine about someone dying is one thing. Potentially witnessing someone die is another. This is all a little too heavy for a Saturday night."

  "Piss off and go get the next girl drunk," I shouted as he so brazenly wondered off. "Mum," I said much more authoritively. "We need to go and get Uncle Dave now."

She nodded before we both rushed towards the direction of our family caravan. I can't remember the last time I'd run so fast. I don't think I'd ever seen Mum run at all.

Concerned as to what I may witness within those caravan walls, I ensured that Mum was first through the door. I don't know what my mother saw in the lounge area exactly but her reaction was enough to make me not want to follow. "Fuck, Dave," she screamed. "Red card!"

I realised amidst all of this chaos just how dysfunctional my family were. The one person we really needed right now was Dad but he wasn't here. He'd have known exactly what to say and do but we were on our own - we had to play with the cards we'd been dealt. It was down to us to try and talk Aiden out of committing suicide. No easy task with Mum, who was completely mangled on whatever she'd taken this evening. There was me - who had the special ability of winding up my brother, simply by being near him. And then there was Uncle Dave, who was... well, Uncle Dave.

God help us.

Chapter Ten: The Day before Happys - Jill's (Mum's) Story

Losing friends over the years is inevitable. It's rarely personal, but as our lives change and priorities change with them, naturally, you lose and gain people throughout the journey.

Chances are though, you have that one person who probably shouldn't be in your more inclusive, adulthood circle of friends, but there they are. You outgrew them a long time ago and you no longer have anything in common, but they still call. They still turn up at your door. They still set you up on dates because it's what they think you need.

Karen is that friend and somehow, I'd once again allowed her to talk me into joining her and two single men for dinner and drinks.

This was the fourth time in just six months she'd managed to do so.

I wasn't opposed to the idea of dating - God knows I'd made my way through many male distractions in recent months. The problem was with the type of men that Karen would try to set me up with.

The first date was with Barry, who brought along a cage containing his pet cat. Apparently, if Tibbles didn't like me - or any woman - a relationship wouldn't be an option. As confident as I was that the feline was freaking out as a consequence of a blind man's dog being close to our table, I was more than happy for Barry to assume that I was an awful, devil woman that he couldn't be with. Next up was Nick, who snuck his own booze into the restaurant. That alone did not actually put me off. It was when he revealed a wrapped up sponge cake in his pocket - his dessert - that I knew it was game over. I never actually met one of the setups, Steven, but after he requested that Karen move the date to an alternative bar that wasn't within one hundred-feet away from a school - for legal reasons - I surmised that it was for the best that we never became acquainted.

Karen and I arrived at the restaurant nice and early - upon my request. It was an opportunity to thoroughly quiz her for more information about our dates. This would allow me to make a quick getaway before their arrival, should I find it appropriate to do so.

With time to kill, we stood in the bar area. It was the first time I'd ever been to this venue, so I took a moment to admire my surroundings. There were a few tell-tale signs that this restaurant was far posher than our usual hangouts. There was complimentary bread at each table and yet not one of the families were fighting amongst themselves to try and get the extra roll. Also, to my amazement, there wasn't a chef sat at the bar with a beer in hand - glaring at us as if to say, *"Don't even think about making me work right now."* The television above the bar wasn't advertising two pitcher cocktails for a tenner or short-skirt Sunday - a promotion I once saw that offered a free shot to anyone in a short skirt. This establishment was instead tuned into the 24-hour news, and the news anchor was currently discussing the murder of a woman that lived just a few miles away - her husband was the main suspect.

The biggest indicator that this restaurant was far too posh for the likes of us, was the extortionate price of a drink.

"Remember, this is my treat," Karen reassured me, picking up on my shock upon seeing how much a drink would cost. "After all, I'm celebrating."

"Indeed... and congratulations on the new job. You'll do great."

Karen pointed at a bottle of wine that for the best part, cost the same as my monthly salary. Even if she could afford it, I felt it would have been wasted on my pallet - given that I'd downed two glasses of cheap cider just an hour ago. I stressed, "You can't order that. It's way too expensive!"

The barman leant it to look at the bottle my friend was pointing at. "Yeah, you can't order that," he chipped in.

Karen looked insulted.

"What is this, Pretty Woman?" she snarled. "You don't know what I can or can't afford!"

The barman looked embarrassed before confirming, "I meant we're out of stock with that particular bottle. Perhaps I can pour you two complimentary glasses of something similar... as you're celebrating?"

"Yes... that would be lovely... thank you," Karen replied in a much softer and humbled tone.

The barman gave me a subtle wink whilst pouring our drinks. He seemed very much my type - certainly in the looks department. He was tall, dark and handsome. Such a cliché, I know but he also seemed kind. Defusing an awkward situation in the way he did was just so lovely. Why couldn't Karen ever set me up with a man like this? I knew my date this evening would once again be the polar opposite.

"So, come on, tell me about the guy you're setting me up with this time," I said wearily.

"His name is James and h-"

"You told me this morning that his name was Daniel?"

Karen looked at me, riddled with guilt.

"Our original dates cancelled on us this afternoon," she admitted. "However, I've organised us two new dates."

Already, I knew this evening was going to be just as much of a disaster as the others. "And what can you tell me about my new date?" I sighed. "Because I'm just dying to know what kind of guy is available on a Friday night with just a few hours' notice?"

"His name is James. Fifty-four. Enjoys fun."

"Right... surely everybody enjoys fun?" I pointed out frustratingly. "The question is, what does James consider to be fun? Selling women's kidneys on the Black Market? Playing Monopoly from the comfort of his cage in the basement, perhaps?"

Confusion hit me. "Also, why did you describe my date like you were reading straight from some online bio?"

Karen couldn't look me in the eyes.

"Seriously?" I sighed. "James is from Kinky Winky, isn't he?"

Karen nodded, still refusing to meet my eyes.

I have limited knowledge of the fetish website Karen had joined a few years ago. She once described 'Kinky Winky' as a casual/zero-drama way for adventurous people to meet and explore their sexual desires. I wasn't being judgemental, but this particular way of meeting men simply wasn't for me. Murders are very much within the realm of possibility, with the recent murder in our city being the prime example of these things not just happening in movies. I dare say that murderers also like to go dating and if I were to bet on the type of dating app they'd be using... I'd most definitely assume it'd be Kinky Winky.

I stressed, "I thought you said you were going to delete your account and explore new hobbies instead?"

"I did delete it... and even attended a few art classes but then I signed up again. It turns out that I really like both painting and penis'," my potentially, soon-to-be ex-friend explained. "I'm not asking you to marry this guy or even sleep with him. I just know how much you need a distraction this weekend. I'll literally be training a few minutes down the road from you at Happys... but if you're adamant that I don't join you, at least give me tonight to try and help. Look... at any point this evening, give me the word and I promise you we'll pack up and leave - no questions asked. All I ask is whilst we are here, we try to make it work. Is that fair?"

This was probably the smartest, most logical thing Karen had ever said to me. I made a mental note of those words for when Aiden or Tracey would inevitably complain about our weekend away - minus the part about sleeping with men. "Okay... fair enough," I responded reluctantly. "Be honest though, have you actually met one decent guy from this kinky site?"

"Actually, yes. There's one guy I'm a little bit smitten with. He's creative - an inspiring author. I read the first few pages of his book and they were shit – really awful - but he's at least trying. The guy is adventurous - said he could probably climb Everest if he put his mind to it, and I believe he could. He'd definitely unintentionally kill himself at some point up there, but, again, he'd give it a go."

"So why is this one not joining us tonight?"

"I started talking about the potential of a relationship between us and he freaked out. He's stood me up the last three times we were supposed to meet since then - last minute stage fright, apparently. He wants to hang out tomorrow. Claims he's even ready to settle. I don't buy it though, so I'm keeping my options open."

"You've given him three more chances than I'd have given."

"Karen, darling," called out an annoyingly brash, cocky, male voice from a distance.

I turned to see an over-confident, skinny man, suited up like a late 19th century London gangster. He strutted over to Karen for a hug and kissed her on each cheek before gracing me with the same greeting. His breath reeked of cigarettes and cheap whisky.

"I'm Carl," he said to me. "And this fine fellow here, is James."

James was of a similar build to Carl, but certainly different when it came to style. Whilst Carl looked like he was desperate to be a cast member for Peaky Blinders, James went with a much more casual look, with bright white jogging bottoms and a matching coloured vest. These clothes told me a lot about the man I was being set up with - such as what he had eaten for lunch, because he was bloomin' covered in splashes of marinara sauce. His unwelcome hug and kiss confirmed my suspicions of a meatball sub lunch.

I should have just been grateful it wasn't splashes of blood. I wouldn't have put it past him, when I considered Karen's track record of setups.

The stale meatball stench was closely followed with a dose of reality. This is not where I should have been this evening. These were not the people I should have been investing my time in. Not tonight. Not this weekend.

I should have been at home.

I looked at the time displayed on the news report. It was already too late for me to pick up my son from his first solo-counselling session but, if I was quick, maybe I could get to have a few words with him before he settled down for the night.

"Let's go order," I instructed, looking to Karen. "Straight to mains... don't worry about starters or dessert." At this point I didn't even care if I sounded rude. I just wanted the evening to be over.

After signalling for our waitress to return to our table barely a minute after seating us, I ambitiously stated, "I think we're all good to order now."

Karen hadn't even opened her menu but for all of her dating faults, she wasn't stupid, so she quickly clicked that I'd already had enough of this date. She subtly gave me a supportive nod before rapidly skimming through the choices.

"What's the quickest meal to prepare?" I asked the waitress impatiently.

"Salad, I guess?"

"I'll have a salad."

"Caesar salad?"

"If a Caesar salad is quick, sure. Heck, just bung the whole iceberg lettuce on a plate if it saves time."

Next up to order was Carl. "Rump steak," he said.

"How would you like your steak cooked?"

Before he even had a chance to answer, I jumped in "Rare!" Not only are well-cooked steaks sacrilege, they take a good ten to fifteen minutes longer to prepare. I couldn't risk this. Carl didn't look impressed but politely confirmed, "Rare would be great... thank you."

"I'll go for the spaghetti and meatballs," James said hesitantly. "If that's okay with you, Jill?"

I think he was being sarcastic but I nodded approvingly, regardless.

Finally, Karen wasted no time getting her order in. "I will also have the salad," she said. "Also, a bottle of the cheapest house white and two beers... also the cheapest."

Karen gave me a comforting smile before continuing supportively, "We'll celebrate properly another weekend. It's alright."

I felt awful but I knew that shortening the date was better than abandoning it completely.

I'm not entirely sure what the topic of conversation was during the first few minutes. I was too busy staring at the clock on the television - envisioning what my family would be doing around this time.

I became distracted further by the image of the man featured in the news report. It was of the suspected wife killer that the police were frantically on the hunt for. I was horrified just how much the man on the screen looked like my date, James. Seriously, they could have been twins. Worse yet... what if my date was the actual killer?

My hands started to shake, overwhelmed by fear and I could feel the adrenaline begin to course through my veins. Had we not have been in such a public place, I'm not sure I'd have had the courage to ask, "So, James... have you ever been married?"

The entire table looked at me as if to suggest my question was perhaps rather forward - or a little out-of-place compared to the light-hearted small talk I'd just interrupted.

Nobody looked more taken aback - suspicious even - than James himself.

"I... was, yes" he confirmed, nervously. "Have you?"

"*How dare you ask such a personal question*," is what I'd have likely of said if it weren't for the fact I'd brought up the subject. So, fair enough.

I didn't respond though. Instead, I eagerly continued my interrogation.

"Where is she now?"

James paused for a few moments before timidly responding, "Last I knew, she was down under."

"Down under... the patio?"

"Down under... Australia."

James was staring right at me. He was absolutely identical to the mugshot being shown on the news. It was a serious and intense glare that sent shivers through my spine. This side-by-side comparison gave me zero doubt that I was indeed sat right next to an actual killer. Karen had truly outdone herself with this pairing.

I could see in James' eyes that he knew I was onto him. I mean, I was being pretty obvious to be fair. I could and should have been more subtle with my questioning. I'd been spending way too much with my unsubtle brother-in-law in recent times.

I couldn't believe that I was in this surreal situation. My heart was in my mouth.

"I just need to use the bathroom... if you'll please excuse me," I tried to sound calm, as if all was fine. Instead, it came out like a terrible child actor over-delivering their lines in a shitty school play.

Once I was in the bathroom, the panic came in full force and I began to hyperventilate. "*What the fuck am I going to do?*" I frantically tried to think of a solution, whilst I leant on the mirror in front of me, struggling to control my breathing.

Pacing back and forth within the confined space of the ladies' toilets, I concluded that this wasn't a situation I should be handling personally. This was a matter for the police and I needed to get them on the phone and persuade them they needed to get here - sooner rather than later.

My plan was to casually head back to the table, grab my phone and excuse myself again - explaining that I needed to call my children. I would then come back here to make the call to the appropriate authorities.

I put on the bravest face I could muster before walking back. What I hadn't planned on, was seeing James walking towards me. "*He's just innocently heading to the loo too,*" I prayed to God. I faked a polite smile before side-stepping to let him past. He simultaneously stepped aside with me. It quickly became apparent he was stopping me in my tracks.

"It's obvious you recognise me," he said, quiet but stern. "Clearly, you know about my wife. How about we just get this dinner over with, go our separate ways and don't mention this encounter to anyone?"

My nerves were threatening to induce vomiting now.

I slowly backed away from the monster. Each time I did so, he did the same toward me, denying me the distance I wanted and moving even closer towards me.

"Step the fuck away from me or I'll scream!" I nervously warned him.

I felt as if someone started grabbing me from behind, pulling me to the floor. I screamed.

It took a few moments to work out that I had, in actual fact, walked backwards into the dessert trolley. I lay, covered from head to toe in icing. The entire restaurant was staring at me, bemused.

Karen rushed over, concerned. "Jill, are you okay?" she scanned me, looking for potential injuries.

I pointed at the news before directing my finger at James. "It's him," I shouted breathlessly. "He's the wife killer!"

James looked freshly bamboozled, which I must confess, created a bit of doubt in my mind.

Karen looked at the screen before leaning in towards me. "Sweetie, they arrested the wife killer this morning," she whispered to me. I could tell she was trying not to display any embarrassment, given my outburst.

James laughed before adding, "Okay, I see what's happened here. I have been told a fair few times that I look like that monster."

I was so confused. This can't have been a misunderstanding. "You said how I clearly knew about your wife!"

James playfully rolled his eyes. "My wife isn't dead," he laughed. "She just doesn't know that I'm out with another woman. I was worried you might have known her and were tempted to blow my cover."

Karen chipped in, "See... he's not a murderer. He's just an asshole."

I felt so stupid. "I'm done with this evening," I sighed, feeling defeated.

I awkwardly made my exit - but not before grabbing our bottle of wine as a consolation prize so as I could at least have a wind-down drink on my way home.

I hadn't been this relieved to walk through my own front door in quite a while. This may sound harsh but I mostly looked for any excuse to be anywhere but at home with the family. Hear me out. My kids are smart; they're headstrong. Simply put, they are better off without me being around them. I had a tendency to make bad situations even worse.

This being said, I felt I at least owed it to Aiden to show my face, following his first solo counselling session. I wouldn't say much - if anything at all - I would just show him that I was around if he needed me.

With the wine bottle in my hand, I headed up the stairs, passing my brother-in-law half way. "I hope you're hungry?" Dave asked.

"Starving," I replied. After all, I never did get to eat the salad I'd made such a big song and dance about in the restaurant.

"Good," he responded. "There's a burger sitting in the microwave but I'm afraid I burnt the chips and had to bung them in the bin."

"You ate them whilst dishing up, didn't you?"

"...Yes."

This must have been the twelfth time I'd heard him use this excuse.

I continued to make my way to the man of the hour. I needed to know that my little princess was okay.

As I opened Aiden's door, he looked me up and down, startled by my appearance. Ah yes, I'd forgotten that I was wearing half of a dessert trolley.

I was also taken aback by what lay before me. Crushed cardboard boxes were scattered around where his bed had previously been. "I don't want to know what happened," I said, fearing that the explanation could cause either Aiden or myself further distress that neither of us needed right now.

"Good, because I really don't want to talk about it," he sighed.

I couldn't wait any longer before asking, "How was today's session?"

"I don't want to talk about that either if you don't mind. What happened to you?"

I laughed. I felt that Aiden might appreciate the full story one day. Not this weekend though. "You wouldn't believe me if I told you," I simply said before taking a sip of the much needed wine. "But you'll likely be pleased to know that my night went very badly."

"What? No." He said trying to hide his smirk. The lying bastard.

I took another sip from the bottle. Even without seeing my son at this very moment, I could sense the judgement.

"You don't want a glass for that?" he asked.

"No, I'm good. It goes down the same hole either way."

I felt this was the time to retreat. It had been a rather pleasant exchanging of words that inevitably would have gone south fast, had I of stuck around.

I opted to finish my wine in bed - perhaps before opening a second bottle for dessert.

As I lay there on the sheets, I didn't know whether to laugh or cry. I was still truly mortified by the situation that had unfolded this evening. At least it was one heck of a distraction.

A moving figure caught my eye. My husband, David, was stood beside the door. "You scared the crap out of me" I laughed. This clearly tickled him too.

I patted the bed sheets with my hand before asking, "You want to join me tonight? We can just cuddle?"

"I wish I could," he replied softly.

"Me too," I sighed. "Before you go though… I need you to believe me when I tell you that I am trying my best."

"I know," my husband croaked.

Fighting back the tears, David gave a smile before walking away.

I couldn't believe it had been almost one year since he had died. It felt like so much longer.

Ever since that horrific evening, I had seen him every single day - stood around as if he were right next to me - for real. I could even hear his voice. It just wasn't enough. I'd have given anything for one more kiss. One more touch.

I know the kids often imagined seeing him too. I'd often hear them talking to their father - seeking advice or comfort.

I downed the rest of my wine, willing the pain to be swallowed down with it.

I missed him so much. We all did.

Chapter Eleven: Another Distraction - Jill's Story

Getting drunk for me, was similar to the spinning of a roulette wheel. It was always a gamble as to what the end result would be. The goal was to numb my pain or simply pass out early in the evening - shortening an undoubtedly difficult day.

Other times though, the drink would heighten the level of pain I was feeling. During these particularly challenging times, I would usually distract myself with the company of men - often pompous, self-centred and one-track minded guys. You know the type.

I'd willingly gravitate towards men that I sensed wouldn't call or even bother to shoot a text the next day, which was fine - by then I would have gotten what I needed from them anyway.

My counsellor would often refer to my actions as self-sabotaging behaviour. Maybe so, but for now, it served a purpose and I was okay with it.

I sound awful, right?

Look, believe it or not, I work ridiculously hard at trying to be the best mother I can possibly be. I'm simply better suited at the behind-the-scenes stuff. For example, there's always food in the house, my kids' clothes are always clean - as are the kids' themselves, I ensure their homework is always completed and I even recently discarded anything within our household that could potentially harm Aiden upon discovering that he'd been having dark thoughts lately. Granted, I'm not the best at talking to my kids' about their feelings - particularly in regards to the loss of their father - but I provide them with a trained professional that they can speak to on a weekly basis.

From an outsider's point-of-view, some would argue that leaving my children to distract themselves at Happys was irresponsible. I would stress that Tracey is fifteen and Aiden, seventeen. They haven't wanted to hang out with their mother on holiday for the last three years - so, why start now? The whole point of this weekend was for things to feel as close to normal as possible.

I did, however, invite Dave along to help keep an eye on things. Some would also find fault that having another adult tag along didn't justify me getting drunk and doing my own thing, to which I would say, *"Piss off!"*

Before you judge me and make your assumptions, try walking a mile in my shoes. I read that recently on Karen's Facebook page. I liked it.

By 8pm on the first day of our weekend away, I was - as one might have guessed - hammered. Plastered. Wasted. Smashed. Basically, very drunk.

Earlier in the day I'd been flirting with the barman and had decided then who this evening's distraction would be. He was named Gary... Gary something. I forget his surname. Gary was toned and it was glaringly obvious that he worked out. His passion for fitness, alongside the job he had, was all I really knew about him.

He'd served me my drinks earlier at the welcome event. The prolonged eye contact, a couple of winks - I assume in case I'd missed the first - and the not so subtle grazing of my hand made it very clear he was interested in me. Well... he was interested in a woman with a pulse at the very least. I'd seen him unsuccessfully try his moves on another female barely a few seconds before trying them with me, but that was fine. I was no stranger to the odds game – essentially this would mean he'd try his luck with as many women as possible before one eventually took the bait. I had no problem with that either. I wasn't looking for a knight in shining armour - an idiot in tin foil would suffice, for now.

Once the back and forth flirting was mutually given and received, Gary and I arranged to have some drinks at the Happys outdoor bar, once he'd finished his shift.

A long thirty or forty minutes later than arranged, he eventually turned up, greeting me with alcoholic drinks in hand and a kiss on each cheek. His breath was potent enough to have knocked me out. He'd already been drinking hard liquor. He passed one of his drinks over to me. I knew straight away there was Whisky in the glasses, and a lot of it. Someone seemed eager to get me drunk. The jokes on him - I was already steaming. Bladdered. Mullered...

"Sorry I'm late," he said half-heartedly. "Some of the team fancied drinks after work so I stuck around for a while."

"That's fine," I lied. Nothing about it was remotely fine actually.

With each passing minute that I'd waited for this jerk, I felt a little more degraded. His bullshit of an excuse didn't help - if anything, it made me feel worse. Had Gary been asked to work longer, fair enough. Or, if a child had been choking, close to death and needed his medical assistance, brilliant - well, a brilliant justification I mean. These reasons and many more would have excused his lateness. The moment I discovered that he'd made the conscious decision not to be on time for such an avoidable and lousy reason, I should have clung on to what little pride I had left and walked away. I didn't.

Gary threw back almost half of his drink before declaring, "This is so out of character for me. I never usually go for drinks with our customers." He was so full of shit.

"I never usually go for drinks with someone I've just met." Yes, I too was full of shit.

"Ya know, the team are off to a beach party shortly with that Lee Lauren bloke. Could be fun, if you fancied it?"

I was quick to dissuade him against this. "If Lee Lauren is there, my daughter will be there too. I'd rather a night away from the kids. Plus, I feel a party for two could be more fun."

Gary seemed both keen and hesitant. "You're right, our own little party does sound more fun," he said. "I didn't know you had kids though."

That right there was, of course, the source of his hesitation. He continued, "What's the situation with their father?"

"I'll put all my cards on the table. I'm not on the lookout for a stepdad and don't worry, there's no crazy ex that's going to hunt you down. I'm simply looking for a guy that can distract me through one of the toughest weekends I'll likely ever live through. Just sex. No feelings. Does that work for you?"

Gary looked flustered. He finished the remainder of his drink before responding, "Yup... I can do that."

"Good."

Unfortunately, the masculine distraction of mine couldn't leave things at that - nice and simple. Curiosity got the better of him before asking, "What's so bad about this particular weekend?"

Gary didn't know this at the time, but he had just cock-blocked himself. I would go on to tell him everything - but by doing so, I'd be ending our date soon afterwards. One of my rules for when choosing guys to have sex with was that they would not, in any way, shape or form, become invested in the details of why I was in so much pain.

I downed my entire glass of cheap booze before explaining, "My husband died one year ago. Let me rephrase that... my husband was *killed* one year ago."

Gary's jaw dropped. "I'm so sorry."

"My son, Aiden, attended a house party with friends. He was instructed to be home by midnight. He was not. Before 12.30am, our boy must have had a dozen missed calls on his phone. By 1am, he still wasn't home and his father and I were pretty pissed off. By 2am, that anger had turned to fear. My husband had initially chosen not to go and confront Aiden in front of his friends to avoid embarrassment, but after being more than two hours late, all pleasantries had expired. It was agreed that Aiden's father would drive over to the house where this party was taking place, before dragging our son home. Even in his worried and furious state, my husband still remembered to kiss me before leaving the house - just as he had always done. This was the last time I saw him alive. That was our last kiss. Aiden has never spoken to me about what happened next. The rest of the details were given to me by the police investigating that evening. My son was late home because he had attempted to walk back and got lost. He had point-blank refused to be driven by Danny Palmer, his friend at the time who was too drunk to walk in a straight-line, let alone drive - but that is exactly what this foolish kid did. Aiden was drunk, but thankfully just sober enough to know that nothing good would come from anyone driving so intoxicated. Quite the understatement. Danny ended up colliding straight into my husband's car at a speed way above the limit. Five people died that evening - the love of my life and four young and naive teens, all of whom still had their whole lives ahead of them. Danny Palmer was the sole survivor... and I really don't know how I feel about that. I guess my thoughts are, that if anyone was to die that night, it should have been him. The worst part is that my son became one of the first witnesses to the aftermath. He put the pieces together way before the emergency services had even arrived - before any adults were there to console him. He was alone... helpless."

It had been a while since I'd told this story. I felt numb.

Gary looked lost for words for a few moments before uttering, "Well... shit."

"Yep. Shit indeed."

He reached into his pocket and pulled out a pill of some sort. "I was gonna take this at the beach party tonight. I think maybe you need it more. It'll fuck you up in the best possible way."

In hindsight, it was such an irresponsible decision but I swallowed the pill without an ounce of hesitation. As Gary was no longer going to be fulfilling his purpose of taking my mind off things, this would have to do.

Predictably, Gary – being the opportunistic sleaze ball he was - jumped on my moment of vulnerability and leant in for a kiss. Meh, why not. Although I had already decided not to sleep with him, I was willing to accept this.

I think we were a good twenty minutes into this teenage-esque snog-a-thon before being interrupted by Tracey. "Mum," she shouted breathlessly.

I felt like a teenager that had just been caught misbehaving. "I... explain," I pleaded with slurred words. I wasn't sure if it was the copious amount of alcohol I'd consumed throughout the day or the pill I'd not long ago popped - either way, my words spoken were not quite in line with my thoughts. I knew that I needed to give my daughter some kind of explanation, but in as fewer words as possible. "He... a man. Me... a woman," I said, totally nailing it - or so I thought at the time.

I could see Tracey wasn't angry or even disappointed. She was worried. In turn, I began to panic too. This was about my son - I just knew it.

"We need to get Uncle Dave, right now," she pleaded. The serious tone confirmed my fears that something serious had happened.

"What... wrong?"

"It's Aiden," she whimpered as tears rushed down her cheeks. These were the words I'd dreaded hearing.

Now in such an emotional state that she could barely get her words out, Tracey simply looked up towards the flats in the distance. I was just about able to make out the silhouette of someone stood at the top of it. Tracey cried, "It's him! I know it! I think he's going to jump!"

Gary grabbed his jacket and stood up, clearly getting ready to leave. He sighed, "Hearing you whine about someone dying is one thing - potentially witnessing someone die is another. This is all a little too heavy for a Saturday night."

What a prick. It seemed Tracey agreed. "Piss off and go get the next girl drunk," she shouted towards him before diverting her attention back to me. "Mum, we need to go and get Uncle Dave now."

I was overwhelmed. In this very moment, I knew I'd let my family down. My daughter was seeking help from Dave as opposed to her own mother and that's when I knew just how bad a state I must have been in.

She was right though. Given the circumstances, he was the best person for the job.

We rushed towards our family caravan. I fought through the burning sensation in my legs and the build-up of sick in my stomach. It was painfully apparent that I needed to up my fitness level rather dramatically.

I crashed through our caravan door and what I saw was almost enough to induce the vomiting.

Over the years, I became increasingly unsurprised by Dave's crazy antics. He surpassed himself in terms of shock value in this moment. "Fuck, Dave - red card!" I screamed whilst bearing witness to my brother-in-law.

Wearing just his underwear, he was tied to the couch with a ball gag in his mouth.

Unable to speak, he was just as shell shocked as I was in this situation.

The moment I removed the gag, he was quick to cry out, "I can explain."

"Later," I responded whilst continuing to release him from his restraints. "Now... Aiden need help."

I was thankful for at least managing to get out the key words but it wasn't enough to stop Dave knowing something was wrong. "Have you taken drugs?" he asked.

"Yes. You... no position to judge. Aiden... need us. He... want to die."

Dave leapt up as soon as he was fully freed. "I need my notebook!"

"Book of filth... no help."

"Trust me, I've written something in there that he needs to read."

I picked up the book of mysteries before passing it over to Dave. "I hope... you know... what you're doing," I said desperately.

"So do I," he muttered.

Chapter Twelve: Let's Get It On - Dave's Story

As I sat helplessly in my underwear, tied to a caravan couch, with a ball gag firmly crammed into my mouth and my sister-in-law witnessing this in utter horror, I thought how this particular scenario could quite easily be listed in my top ten most embarrassing moments, ever.

How did I find myself in this situation? Please allow me to explain.

I am not your average novelist. I'm what you might call a 'method writer'. I do my best to personally experience - first-hand - the scenarios that my characters find themselves in. It's all about authenticity. Allow me to offer you an example: I had an idea a few months back for a fictional story about a man trapped at sea for weeks on end, with nothing but a potato - which would later become his trusted companion. What would be going through this guy's mind to help pass the time? At what point would he eat his new friend in order to survive? Just how wrinkled would his fingers become? I had to know the answers. I'm not great with open water though, so opted for a really, really long bath to conduct my experiment. In total, I must have been sat in there for two full days before I got bored of this idea and moved onto the next.

For those that are curious, I took my first bite into 'Potato Paul' at the five-hour mark. I knew I'd miss him but I was really hungry.

It was in that tub that I started to wonder, *"What is it that the masses love?"* I visualised around two-dozen things, some standing out as more popular than the rest - those being cheese, Freddos (back when they were just 10p per bar) and, of course, porn. Once I'd gathered my research, I knew that the latter would become the sole focus of my next book. Well, my first book.

For almost three decades I've announced on every single New Years Day, "This will finally be the year that I complete a novel." In reality, I'd never make it past a few pages before getting bored and giving up. That had to change.

It pained me that my brother never got to witness me persisting with my personal project all the way to completion. I swore to myself that the rest of the family at least, would see that I was capable of doing it.

My research into pornographic novels revealed that the Fifty Shades of Grey books topped best-seller lists all around the world. There was definitely an audience for this filth but my attempt at the genre had to be different. I needed it to stand out. The unique angle came to me upon seeing a female eating pork scratchings. It dawned on me whilst witnessing this... times had changed. If women were now eating deep-fried, pork bar snacks, maybe it was also time for them to be the dominant leads in erotic novels? It would be a feminist reimagining of the popular 50 Shades series.

There was one big problem... I knew very little about feminism then. Apparently, it wasn't about females burning bra's and hating on men. For my novel to be the best version it could be, I knew I'd have to step up my method writing game. I'd have to actually meet up with modern, open-minded and dominating females in person. Where would I go to find this demographic? An adult app once recommended to me called Kinky Winky.

It was mostly home to people looking for casual, no-strings meetups. Members' bios tended to be refreshingly honest - detailing exactly what they were or weren't looking for. It made my tailored search really quite simple.

Perhaps surprising - given the nature of the app - most of the dates I had resulted in nothing more than conversation. This was often their choice, granted - but sometimes mine. During these chats, I'd often tell them about the book I was writing and they'd usually share their past experiences of being on such a raunchy and notoriously controversial application. Predominantly, the women I met spoke of positive encounters they'd had, but there were definitely a few negative themes emerging that some of these women felt I should consider highlighting in my literature. Many stressed that regardless of how wild or forward they happened to be personally, manners and common courtesy from men went a long way. I was told that, yes, a bio could very well list their interests as the kinkiest stuff imaginable, but that does not necessarily mean that they will want to do these particular things with just any random meetup. Even if sex had been arranged prior, a person can and must be allowed to change their mind - and when that happens, manipulative or pushy behaviour is not tolerated. Finally, in regards to unsolicited dick pics - that shit needs to stop. It makes the sender no better than a creepy pervert opening their duffle coat in public.

I'd like to make it clear that much of what was said to me was not new information. If it all sounded pretty obvious to you too, congratulations, you're probably not a predatory dickhead either.

I enjoyed my time using Kinky Winky. I loved the company of these women. I wasn't used to being on dates with such honest conversation, where all cards were placed on the table from the get-go. It felt like a much more authentic exchange than the dating I had previously grown accustomed to. The moment I decided I was done with it all however, came soon after I unintentionally met up with someone that I knew pretty well from my more conventional life outside of the app.

Most pictures on Kinky Winky would show faces blurred or cropped out for obvious reasons. This was the case for my final meetup who, unbeknownst to me, until our in-person encounter, turned out to be a stunner named Karen - a dear friend of my sister-in-law, who I had seen many a time in passing.

Although we were both embarrassed at this big reveal, we persisted with the drinks we'd planned, regardless. Before the date, we'd only ever made small talk. Thanks to this more intimate one-on-one time, conversation with her suddenly felt different. It was better - more personal. Real. I discovered that she was once married to, in her words, "some wanker". She was also career-driven, with a big interview lined-up in a months' time at a big law firm. Another discovery was that she was really funny - so much so, she managed to make me laugh harder than I do any time I see Melissa McCarthy fall over in her movies.

We both agreed that a second date would be lovely - but that there should be ground rules if we were to continue to see each other. Karen wanted me to promise not to tell Jill about us - certainly not at this point. There was to be no drama, unless her ex had royally fucked up and she therefore needed to rant. And finally, I was to never ask Karen again if she'd like to read some pages of the book I was writing - it was to be assumed that she most definitely would not.

The second date was quickly followed by a third. Within a single week, dates four, five and six had come and gone.

It was during the seventh encounter that Karen casually mentioned how she wouldn't be totally against the idea of a relationship. This was quickly played down as banter after I responded with an awkward, "Yeah... maybe?" Don't get me wrong, I'd thought about it... a lot. I also had no interest in dating anyone else and had even deleted the Kinky Winky app ages ago. A relationship between us made sense and yet the thought of it scared the crap out of me. In my personal experience, the moment things become official is when everything starts going wrong. During the dating phase, you're getting a blow job whilst playing Call of Duty. Then, once in the official phase, the PlayStation is hidden away safely until you learn to put more time into the relationship. Then comes the whining... "Dave, you promised me that we were going to a proper restaurant?!" Well, a quick and simple Google search showed that Maccy D's was, in actual fact, a proper restaurant.

I was the happiest I'd ever been around Karen, but that was with our current arrangement. I didn't want to risk losing what this was.

I'm ashamed to say that I had cancelled on my next few dates with Karen. I'd have every intention of going and genuinely looked forward to it, but at the last minute, I'd freak out and text that I wouldn't be there. I know, I know - what kind of coward doesn't even call? This one.

I was given one final lifeline with this incredibly patient woman. I mentioned to her how I would be spending the weekend at Happys Holidays with Jill, Aiden and Tracey. Coincidentally, Karen was to be less than a mile away at the exact same time, training for her new job. She agreed to meet me over the weekend for a quick drink and chat, but stressed that if I were to back out once again, it would finally be game over for me. That seemed fair.

I text Karen the caravan number with reassurance that the family would all be out by 8pm - making that the perfect time for her to come over. "I'll be there," she responded.

I'd be lying if I said I that the nerves didn't start to pile up just moments later, but I was adamant not to cancel. I had to keep reminding myself that I had agreed to a casual meet and that it wasn't a bloomin' death sentence.

By the time I'd convinced my Niece to leave the caravan for a while, there was just a few minutes left until 8pm. I had somehow completely rearranged the lounge area within that short amount of time in an attempt to create a romantic ambience. Candles warmly lit the room - just bright enough for us to see each other but too dark to see the vomit and semen stains, graciously left by previous guests. For this occasion, I'd even decided I'd extend my normally strict cap of a tenner, when purchasing a bottle of thirteen-pound white wine. It was the least I could do given my shitty behaviour recently. The wine was chilling nicely on the table and the icing on the cake was the sound of Barry White serenading softly in the background.

Right on schedule, there was a knock at the rickety door. "Come in," I called out nervously.

Karen walked in wearing her business attire. She was even carrying a briefcase. It was a good look. Authoritive. Sexy.

"What's in the briefcase?" I asked.

"I'm glad you ask. I figure we probably don't have long together this evening, so let's make every moment count." Opening the case, she continued, "I've brought along some toys. Before I continue with what I came here to do, can you first consent that you are happy to be restrained? You're okay with a gag in the mouth? Basically... are you happy for me to do whatever I came here to do?"

This, I had not expected. Through my excitement, the only words I could muster together were, "I consent."

"Fabulous," she replied, following through with her promise. Within a minute I was restrained, gagged and wearing nothing but my underwear - the very setup I would later be caught in.

I became confused when Karen continued to root through her belongings, pulling out paper and fancy colouring pencils."

I tried to ask, "Sorry, what's happening here?" All that came out though was a muffled sound.

"You're probably wondering what's happening here?" she asked as she began to draw on the paper. "I've had to do a lot of self-reflecting, no thanks to you. What kind of woman gets stood up a good handful of times by the same man and still comes running towards him like a loyal dog the moment he whistles? Someone with low self-esteem and little respect towards herself I've concluded. I liked you, Dave. Like a fool, I still do. Every time I thought of calling you, I turned to art instead. I'm getting really good at it."

Karen held up a sketch of me in this embarrassing situation I'd found myself in. It was pretty good to be fair. She concluded, "I will give you one last chance but not before you get a taste of the embarrassment you've subjected me to on numerous occasions. Stand me up again and I'll proudly display this picture in my lounge as a little reminder that you aren't shit worth even thinking about and when you call or text, I should ignore it. Look at you. Pathetic."

Just seconds later, she was gone and I was more in love with her than I ever was before.

Yeah, it wasn't logical to me either - but now was not the time to analyse. I had to get myself out of this situation before the fami...

Too late.

Jill came barging through the door. She looked understandably confused by the situation sprung upon her. As her eyes searched over each new detail, she become increasingly horrified. "Fuck, Dave! Red card!" she shouted.

I tried to explain how this wasn't quite my fault but the only sounds to come from me were once again desperate muffles.

My sister-in-law removed my ball gag - a sentence I never thought I'd say - and the moment my jaw was free, I cried out, "I can explain!"

"Later," she responded whilst continuing to free me. "Now... Aiden need help."

I wasn't quite sure why she was talking like a cavewoman. Booze had never really affected her in this way. It dawned on me. "Have you taken drugs?" I asked.

"Yes. You... no position to judge," she said looking around the room. "Aiden... need us. He... want to die."

Dammit. The boy and I had discussed his suicidal thoughts just yesterday and he seemed fine.

"I need my notebook!" I explained in a panic.

"Book of filth... no help."

"Trust me, I've written something in there that he needs to read."

Passing me my notes, Jill said, "I hope... you know... what you're doing."

"So do I."

We wasted no more time in rushing towards my Nephew, with Tracey joining us.

Lo and behold, there he was, up on the roof of a tall block of flats.

Once reaching our destination, we pushed past a group of onlookers that had started to gather below to gain entry into the building. Side note - whilst asparagus, oysters and pineapple might make for great aphrodisiacs, they are not the best foods to binge on prior to running up a dozen flights of stairs. By the time we'd reached the top, even Tracey was shattered, so imagine just how defeated her mother and I were - two people twice her age and weight. I can only assume it was the adrenaline that carried us this far.

Aiden looked surprised to see us all climbing onto the roof from an opened hallway window. "Do not come near me," he pleaded. His cheeks were red and puffy. He'd clearly been crying for quite some time.

I used my hands to signal for Jill and Tracey to remain behind me. I felt that it was important we kept our distance as requested.

Aiden continued, "This is one of the reasons why I hate this world. It takes extreme moments like this for people to actually start giving a shit. It's too little, too late - so save your words. I know exactly the kind of bullshit lines you're going to use!"

Jill stood tall and confident before announcing, "Aiden... bye bye... equals me... sad sad."

Aiden stared at his mother, puzzled. "Okay, that... I did not expect to hear."

Now was my time to step up. "I'm not going to bullshit you," I said calmly. "We've been tiptoeing around the elephant in the room throughout every counselling session for almost a year and look where it has gotten us. Aiden, you're ready to give up on life. Then there's me... I'm so desperate to be seen as just half the amazing man your father was - so much so, I lie and I exaggerate, but they're all just empty words. Your mother is a mess. I mean, she's literally high on drugs right now. Then there is Tracey who has brought shame upon this family by becoming a YouTuber."

Tracey understandably looked insulted by this. Jill didn't seem to care though – she was away with the fairies.

"Wait, Mums' on drugs?" Aiden asked bewildered. "Where would you even get drugs at a family resort like this?"

"Gary," Jill and I both said in unison. I added awkwardly, "...so I've heard."

Knowing I'd digressed from the main point, I steered the conversation back in the right direction by continuing, "Look... I'm going to say his name. I'm going to say it because right now, what do we have to lose? David Gardener is gone. He's gone forever and it fucking hurts... so bad. We all feel his loss every single day."

Aiden appeared to be overcome with fury within just a mere second of hearing this. "Try adding that loss with the crippling weight of guilt! Dad would still be here now if it weren't for me. You have no idea how that feels."

Reluctantly, I admitted, "I do, actually. He'd probably still be here if it weren't for me too. He left your family home that night just moments after I text him to say that he should."

Jill added, "David... want me to drive." She took a deep breath and slapped her face in a desperate attempt to increase her focus before slowly continuing, "Your father... thought I should drive... to the party because he... he was angry. I... I did not listen. Now... he gone."

Aiden shook his head disapprovingly. "You feel so guilty that you'll quite happily completely distance yourself from us," he snapped sarcastically. "What kind of mother does that?"

Jill calmly explained, "A mother... a mother that knows... your best qualities... come from your father." Fighting back the tears, she continued, "Me. I. I am scared... of... undoing… his hard work."

The entire family fell silent. This was all a lot of information for us to process. I felt like this was the type of conversation we'd always been encouraged to have during counselling but it never happened. I hoped, so much, that initiating the discussion had been for the best.

It was during this moment of quiet reflection that we could hear the crowds growing bigger and louder from the streets below. "Jump," shouted the distinctive voice of Lee Lauren. What a prick.

I noticed my nephew edging ever so slightly closer, towards the edge. I desperately called out, "There's something I'd like you to see."

I slid my notepad towards Aiden's feet before requesting, "Read page eleven."

He reluctantly flicked through the pages before pausing with a look of disgust. He read out loud, "I took him into my play room. He was excited at the vast array of toys laid out before him - whips, chains, vibrators, lubricants and Goldeneye for the N64." Aiden slammed shut the book before asking, "Why are you showing me this?"

I'd gotten the page wrong. This had honestly not been a desperate attempt at getting the family to read more of my work.

"I meant page fourteen. Please. Just read it," I called out.

Aiden reopened my notes, stopping at the suggested page. He looked even more grossed out than before. Following a heavy sigh, he reiterated my words to the family. "I've had a hundred different girls from a dozen different cities. None of them lived up to your bacon flavoured titties." Aiden looked me dead in the eyes before adding, "What the hell is wrong with you?"

I had once again given the wrong page number. "Fifteen," I shouted confidently. "What I actually want you to read is on page fifteen. I'm certain of it this time."

"I really hope so because what I've read so far has just made me want to jump even more."

Aiden read the words internally this time round. His eyes watered up further and his jaw literally dropped. "Is this how you feel?" he asked softly.

"It is," I replied.

My nephew slowly started to walk towards me. I was relieved to see him away from the edge.

"It's how I feel too," he said before approaching me for a hug. He gripped me and wept. Jill and Tracey gave a sigh of relief before clinging onto us too.

We remained in that beautifully intimate position for a minute before Aiden said, "Let's get back to the Caravan. I think mum could use a coffee. Maybe a cold shower."

Tracey asked, "Can we maybe stay like this for just one more minute first?"

We continued to hug and it felt incredible.

Tracey then asked curiously, "What's in the book?"

"You'll know soon enough," Aiden responded.

Chapter Thirteen: - The Second Day at Happys - Aiden's Story

I worry far too much about future events. I'll often create scenarios in my mind that play out in the worst ways imaginable, only to find out that in reality, everything would be fine. Not great - but fine. Certainly never as bad as I'd feared.

I was awake in my bed at 3.47am - exactly one year from the moment my father was officially declared dead. I'd feared this anniversary for so long.

I was acutely aware of the increase in my heartrate, with each second that approached closer to 3.47am. I half expected a grand, supernatural payback of sorts, from beyond the grave and I'm not even kidding when I say that. Of course, the moment the time aligned, to that of the time of my past tragedy, I was fine. Was I sad? Yes, beyond any human measure. Heartbroken? Also, yes, to the extent it felt like a serious, physical injury. But, just like everything else leading up to this moment in time, it was not quite as terrible as I had feared for so long.

It would seem I wasn't the only one in the family who was awake at this time. I could hear the clanging of plates from the kitchen, I headed out of my room to go investigate. Mum was making herself a bowl of cereal. I prepared one for myself and sat beside her at the small dining table.

"I think the drugs have worn off," she said, embarrassed.

"Good." I was relieved to hear a full sentence from her.

"Aiden... did I storm the stage last night to tell the lead singer of Arrr-Ha to walk the plank, before dragging him into the pool?"

"No."

"Thank God for that."

"No... it was the drummer that you dragged into the pool."

Mum looked mortified, uneasy and fidgeted in her seat. "I'm not like other mums, am I?"

"You're not. But that's not always a bad thing."

My mother held my hand. "Everything is going to be better from this point on," she said, supportively.

"I know."

We'd not even taken a bite into our cornflakes when we were joined by Tracey and Uncle Dave, who both got straight to making themselves breakfast. For the first time since my dad had passed, we were sat together as a family by choice - not because counselling had forced us to do so.

I'm not sure you'll be able to fully understand the strength it took for me to do so, but I started to speak about the most incredible man I had ever known. "It always makes me smile when I think about the story Dad once told me about - when you both ordered breakfast to your room at that fancy hotel. Some poor staff member knocked on the door and Dad discovered the hard way that shouting *'coming'* sounds a lot like *'come in'*. In walks this stranger with Dad stood in the middle of the room stark bollock naked," I reminisced, fondly, between escaping giggles.

Mum laughed, "They both just looked at each other, terrified. They must have been embarrassed, but no way near as much as I was after walking in on my brother-in-law, gagged, restrained and wearing nothing but his boxers!"

For the first time in a while, I was not only comfortable being around the family, but we were all laughing together. I dare say they felt the same too. I mean, Tracey didn't even pick up her phone - not even once within the next few hours.

By the time it reached a more traditional waking hour, I had decided there was something I desperately wanted to go and do. I was reluctant at first because a part of me felt I should cling on to this moment for as long as possible. I had to take comfort in knowing that this family gathering would, hopefully, become the new norm again.

I announced to everyone, "I'm going to nip out for a short while. Uncle Dave, do you mind if I borrow your notebook?"

"I guess," he said hesitantly. "Just look after it. There's a lot of good ideas in that book that I don't want people nicking. If I suddenly see cheese toastie machines built into cars, I'll know the leak of my invention had something to do with you."

He passed over his prized possession.

Mum couldn't hold back her concerns. "I think one of us should come with you."

"Honestly… I'll be fine."

After a few moments of deep thought, she softly replied, "Okay. I love you." I could hear the uncertainty in her voice but I could appreciate her anxiety.

"I love you too."

Walking through the Happys resort, I was finally able to feel the vibrant energy I'd experienced there in previous years. In the pool, families were having lilo races, which consisted of lining up a bunch of inflatables and seeing how far you could run across them before face planting into the water. Just across from that activity were two young girls working on a dance routine - I assume in preparation for the talent show later in the day. I could also see the sweetest elderly couple exercising in the sun. My bad - upon further inspection, they were leaning for their 8am cans of lagers - and fair play to them. There was a common theme amidst the pockets of strangers. They all looked incredibly happy. It was borderline inconceivable to think that I was stood in the exact same place I'd spent time in just yesterday. I was so focused on negatives; I didn't allow any space to recognise the positive things surrounding me - other than Alizia. In fairness, how could I not have noticed somebody so perfect? As was tradition for me though, I truly messed up what might have been with her.

With Uncle Dave's notebook safe in my hand, I returned to the beach and sat near the spot where the party had been hosted the night before.

I started to mull things over a bit and I discovered a flaw within myself - I never learn. I had once again fallen victim to Hollywood's ideology of this being the perfect surrounding for me to self-reflect. The picturesque view of the open water and the sound of foaming salt water, as waves journeyed backwards from the pebbled shore, was soothing - I can't argue that. But the seemingly perfect ambience was rather muddied by the empty beer bottles, a dog crapping on a discarded, crumbled sandcastle and the unconscious mystery man who had the penis drawn onto his face, still exactly where he'd been last night. I admired the level of detail and shading that had been added since I last saw him, though I couldn't help but feel concern for his wellbeing. Just as I was about to check in on him, a random girl sat on the sand beside me.

The stranger was gorgeous - blonde hair, soft eyes and a petite frame. Naturally, I wondered what kind of con was in store for me. Nobody this attractive would be approaching me unless there was some kind of hidden agenda, after all.

The mysterious girl said, "I also thought this would be a good spot to come and reflect on life." Her voice was eerily familiar. She continued, "But, within seconds of walking on the sand barefoot, a used condom got wedged between my toes. Totally ruined the vibe. You don't see that in the movies."

Firstly, disgusting. Secondly, I definitely knew that voice. "Wait... Alizia?" I was beyond confused.

"The one and only," she confirmed.

It would seem she had gone through one of those makeup face transformations I'd seen in her videos - but with this particular effort eclipsing any previous attempts I had seen. "If it weren't for the voice, I never would have known it was you," I said impressed - though still puzzled.

"Turns out my own Fiancé didn't recognise me either. Sorry... ex fiancé."

Hearing this revelation unintentionally brought a huge smile to my face - probably not very supportive. I concentrated and unskilfully turned my smile into a frown.

"What are you doing with your face? You look mental," Alizia continued.

"I'm sorry."

"You're not. But that's okay. So many people had tried warning me about Lee but I didn't want to hear it. I guess ignorance can be bliss."

"What happened?" I asked, sincerely worrying if she was alright.

"We saw you on that rooftop last night."

"Great." I hung my head, feeling exposed.

Alizia continued, "Lee found the whole situation hilarious. He even shouted for you to jump."

"Yeah... I heard him."

"He was showing off - but regardless, I was disgusted. I didn't think he was like that. I started to question what else I didn't know about the man I was going to marry. Ya know, I'd often get private messages from girls claiming they'd slept with him. Of course, he'd always say these people were nothing more than jealous fans trying to get five minutes of fame and that he would never cheat on me. I had to know for sure. So, after he continued his evening at some nightclub without me, I returned to our caravan to quite literally put on a new face whilst working on a cute little Irish accent to go with it. I made a move on him a little while later and that bastard didn't even hesitate to drag me to a more private area to kiss who he believed to be a complete stranger."

"Well... fuck," I said, unsure of what a socially acceptable response was in this situation.

"I can't believe I came off my socials for that prick. He never actually asked me to, granted, but what he did was arguably worse. I couldn't post anything without his judgemental shadow leering over me. He was always there, demanding to know why I felt the need to say certain things and who it was aimed for - like it was any of his business. It grew tiresome really quick so I just stopped. I came off all of it."

Still lost for appropriate words, I couldn't help but say something that was burning at the forefront of my mind. "Perhaps this isn't the right time to ask this," I said sensitively. "But... can I hear the Irish accent?"

Alizia stared at me, annoyed. It was a look that screamed, *"You insensitive tosser!"* I felt awful. The awkward moment I'd created persisted for a few brutal seconds before she burst out laughing. I had yet again fallen victim to her dry humour.

"Sure... one sec," she said whilst stretching her jaw - bracing herself for the performance. In a voice that was possibly the worst attempt at an Irish accent I'd ever heard, she said, "I like to drink Guinness all day with my leprechaun."

"That was terrible," I teased. "And quite possibly racist."

"It really is bad, right? Luckily the music drowned out just how awful it is." Alizia paused and then, in a more serious tone, went on, "I probably should have done more to help when it looked like you were going to jump from that building. You have to keep in mind, at the time I saw you as an idiot. You had not long ago punched Lee Lauren and I felt a loyalty to him."

"And what do you see me as now?"

With the cutest smirk, she responded, "A little bit of a legend. After all, you punched Lee Lauren."

Alizia gave me a wink that made my heart flutter before continuing, "I caught a glimpse of Lee filming a breakfast scene in the restaurant this morning. He used anything and everything around him to cover his face - napkins, the menu, plates - you name it. If it was there, he was using it to hide his bruises. It was kinda satisfying and funny to watch. Is that harsh?"

"No. You're just being honest."

"So, if you don't mind me asking, what made you consider jumping?"

I felt like my conversation with the family this morning about dad was the apt warmup for this conversation.

"I don't mind." I'm almost certain that I genuinely meant it too. "My dad died one year ago today."

Just like that, I'd said it out loud for the first time since it had happened. Again, the thought of this moment had been far worse in my mind than the actual reality. The ground didn't crumble below me; my heart didn't explode. I was fine.

"I'm so sorry," Alizia said whilst placing her hand on my knee. This had truly become a bittersweet moment.

"I blame myself. He was out looking for me when it happened" I elaborated. "But… I also forgive myself. It took 365 days but I got there."

With her hand still on me, Alizia reassured, "I've no doubt your father would have wanted you to forgive yourself much sooner."

"It's true. He was very much about living life to the fullest. At his funeral, they played 'My Way' by Frank Sinatra over a photo and video montage playing on a big screen. He had lived a colourful life. He'd climbed the highest mountains, swam the deepest seas and was never afraid to say yes to any opportunity presented to him if he felt it'd make an interesting pub story. You could argue that the choice of song played at his funeral was rather cliché, but fuck me was he worthy of it. I recently wondered, if I were to have 'My Way' played at my own funeral, what pictures or videos would I want to be shown of myself? There's none. I've wasted my life. I'm simply not worthy of Sinatra being played when I die."

"One last time," Alizia said. "You're definitely seventeen and not seventy?"

I could see the point she was trying to make.

My crush continued, "The last twelve months must have been hell but you still have your whole life ahead of you. You are going to be presented with so many opportunities in your lifetime and should you want them, you grab them. Seize the moment."

I was almost certain I knew what Alizia was hinting at. The look she was giving me pretty much confirmed it. Seizing the moment, I went in for a kiss and she... retracted. It's the reaction everyone fears before going in for the first kiss. Needless to say, I was a bit traumatised by the rejection and felt guilty too. "I'm so sorry," I panicked. "I just figured now that you're not with Lee-"

"...Now that I'm not with Lee, it's probably a good time to focus on myself again?" Alizia interrupted.

"Yes. Of course. You're right." I was so, so embarrassed.

She looked at me in the same way that someone might look at an injured puppy. "Here's the thing," she said sensitively. "I have no reason to be here at Happys today. The only reason I came here in the first place was to support that cheating wanker and despite that relationship being over, here I am. I'd rather be supporting you as you sing in that talent show. That's why I'm sticking around a little longer. But... I'd be supporting you as a friend. Be honest, is that enough?"

I felt awful. Alizia was probably inundated with guys trying their luck with her. She deserved more than some douchebag trying it on - especially at such a vulnerable time. "A friendship with you is way more than enough," I said sincerely.

"Good."

An uncomfortable silence was interrupted by the guy with a penis drawn on his head, giving out a groan. It sounded like he was in pain as he slowly staggered up onto his feet - and just like that, the drunk stranger was hobbling away, still appearing to be quite drunk. "Thank God," I said. "I was starting to think he was dead."

I was thankful for whoever he was for having provided us with a much needed change of tone. Alizia and I continued to talk in the playful way we had been - prior to me almost fucking everything up.

"I can't wait to hear that cookie song again," she said excitedly.

"Actually, I had another song in mind."

"Oh, really? Tell me more."

I held up Uncle Dave's notebook before explaining, "My Uncle wrote a song yesterday. It beautifully illustrates how he's felt since our loss. I attempted to write a song myself this weekend around the same subject, but I couldn't find the words. Turns out, I didn't need to. Uncle Dave managed to put into words exactly what I'd been struggling to say."

"So... you're going to perform your uncle's song?"

"I think so, yeah. Any chance I can borrow your guitar again?"

"Of course," Alizia squealed, even more excited than before. In her awful Irish accent, she continued, "This is going to be craic."

"If we're going to be friends, you have got to stop the accent," I teased.

"Yeah... that's fair."

Chapter Fourteen: - The Talent Show - Aiden's Story

Happys' Talent Show was in full swing. Currently on stage was a young girl whose act was simply pretending to be on the moon. She was walking back and forth across the length of the stage as slowly as she could. It was ridiculously cute.

I grew increasingly nervous waiting for my time to shine - or, more likely - time to humiliate myself. Thankfully, I was in great company and therefore, distracted enough that I wasn't overthinking and working myself up about the upcoming performance. As if by a miracle, I hadn't scared Alizia away with my presumptuousness earlier in the day. She had chosen to sit with Tracey and I to watch the show. We'd been sat in the hall together for about thirty minutes and all three of us were thoroughly enjoying ourselves. Between acts, we were laughing aloud and the conversation flowed effortlessly between us. The air of pleasantness was aided by my sister being... how to put this... normal. I had feared she might have been overbearing in the real life company of an online influencer, especially someone she admired so much, but she played it really cool - not even squealing once.

Sat in front of us, close to the stage, were the talent show judging panel, who consisted of the Taylor Twins and Lee, who did not look impressed that I was sat with his ex. He kept peering across in our direction, with a look that I'm quite certain would actually kill... if it weren't for the fact his face was smothered in makeup. Presumably, this was an attempt to hide the bruises that I had left.

Did I regret causing him harm? You might be surprised to hear that, actually, yes. He played a huge part in stirring the overwhelming rage I had experienced but ultimately, only I am to blame for my own actions. Lee was an absolute dick last night but so was I. Only by acknowledging that fact and owning that I had my own part to play, can I learn and grow from it.

Also watching the show from a few tables left of ours, were Mum, Uncle Dave and – oddly - Karen. I guess I shouldn't have been too surprised to see Mum's friend swing by as I'd seen her post to Facebook just a few hours earlier that she was in the area. I'm telling you, if she ever had a stalker, she'd make their job tremendously easy, as Karen can't bloody go anywhere without needing to provide the whole world with every little detail.

It might have seemed odd to an outsider that my family weren't all sat together. I honestly preferred it this way. Sitting at breakfast in their company this morning was lovely and it was reminiscent of how things were before Dad had died. That being said, living in each other's pockets all of the time had never been our thing though, so why start now?

The young girl on stage had now been walking slowly for about eight minutes. Tommy Taylor took it upon himself to declare the act was over. "Give it up for Gemma with her impression of an astronaut," he said on the mic. As the audience applauded, Tommy continued, "Up next is the young rapper, Lil Problemz."

Tracey looked at me with the biggest grin. "You'll be up next," she said excitedly. "I know," I replied, now starting to feel physically sick with nerves.

If Lil Problemz was nervous, he hid it well. As soon as the confident young boy took to the stage, he owned it. Grabbing the mic, there was zero hesitation before he began rapping.

"Salad for dinner, mum?
This ain't a farm.
I'm on the phone to child protection,
raising the alarm.
Darren's having pizza.
He'll probably get his own dip.
It's been more than a week since I even had a chip.
An apple for dessert? That ain't even sweet.
Sort it out. Go get me something else to eat.
If anyone can relate, go and give my page a like.
I'm Lil Problemz and it's time to drop the mic."

Remembering he'd gotten into trouble the last time he dropped the microphone, the boy lowered it to about half an inch above the ground before releasing it.

The audience once again showed their appreciation towards the acts, and my heart pounded faster and harder. I'd performed to much bigger crowds compared to this, but never with a song so personal and I knew how out of practice I'd gotten.

Lee took the mic from Tommy, declaring to the room, "We next have Aiden Gardener... singing his pedo song."

I knew he was trying to get a rise out of me again. This time I was not going to take the bait. Instead, I grabbed Alizia's guitar and marched over to the stage with a forced smile. I could see my family, Alizia and Karen all cheering. It was comforting.

I wasted no time in grabbing the stage mic before announcing, "I'll actually be singing a new song and it was written by my uncle."

Uncle Dave looked pleasantly surprised by this revelation. "Yeah.... Bacon flavoured titties," he shouted proudly before giving out a *"whoop"*.

A second whoop came from the bar area. It was none other than the Speedo guy. He was still proudly sporting the teeny, tiny swimwear.

"I'm sorry to disappoint," I said. "This is my Uncle's *other* song."

My hand began to shake with the endlessly increasing nerves. There was no way I would be able to play the instrument in this state. I tried to imagine that I was about to perform to an empty room. I'd just about managed to visualise row upon row of empty seats but no matter how hard I tried, there was one person I just couldn't make disappear... my dad. He looked towards me proudly - just as he did every time he'd seen me perform in the past.

The shaking became more manageable and I knew it was now or never. "This is for you, Dad." Strumming on the guitar, I began to sing,

"The days are long until I see you again.
Each waking hour filled with loneliness and pain.
You give me strength until the sun goes down,
knowing then I'll be asleep and that you'll be around.
We will talk about what's happening with me.
The closest thing to how things used to be.
You'll guide me, praise what's right, say what's wrong.
I wake up. The hurt returns. That's when you're gone.

"Don't wake me, please this I pray.
There's another place that I'd rather be.
Don't wake me. Please, not today.
There's just one person that I need to see.
He'll know what to say to make the world seem alright.
Through the darkness, he will always find the light.

"Don't wake me. Please, not today."

The audience responded well to the song - applauding, as they had done for each of the acts. I didn't stick around for very long to truly appreciate the atmosphere though. After handing Alizia back her guitar, I rushed outside to get some air.

It had taken every bit of strength I had to keep it together during the performance. The moment I was alone, the pent-up emotion exploded and my tears erupted.
I was quickly joined by everyone. Mum, Uncle Dave, Tracey, Alizia and Karen all rushed to my aid. I simply couldn't stop the tears. I'd never felt so embarrassed or vulnerable.

Alizia looked deeply into my eyes before softly telling me, "That was beautiful. Your dad would be so proud."

Tracey added, "We're all proud."

"Thank you." As the crying gradually became more manageable, I continued, "Uncle Dave... your words were perfect."

"Personally, I think Bacon Flavoured Titties would have been more of a crowd pleaser," he joked. "But thank you."

I'd been too wrapped up in my own emotions to notice something was out of the ordinary until now. Uncle Dave and Karen were holding hands. "Wait a second," I said confused, whilst pointing at the source of my sudden disconcertment. "What's happening here?"

Mum announced, "Apparently it's been going on for a while."

"And the world is still spinning?" I joked.

"Very funny," Karen said, rolling her eyes. "Almost as funny as when Jill made the exact same joke an hour ago. Now, if we're all done sucking each other's cocks, how about we get some shots before you all head home?"

Uncle Dave perked up. "Hell yes!"

Mum didn't appear quite as sold on the idea. "Actually, you guys drink whatever you like but I think I'll stick to the orange juice."

I was proud. Clearly Mum was taking difficult but positive steps towards a healthier lifestyle.

Or not.

It wasn't long before she retracted her previous statement by conceding, "Actually, I'll have one shot. Maybe two."

To be fair, two shots was still better than an all-day binge. I concluded this was to remain a win.

As the family began to return to the entertainment hall, Alizia was quick to grab my hand, pulling me in for a more private discussion.

"I kind of need to start heading home now," she said, disheartened. "So... goodbye."

"Can we keep in touch?" I asked a little too eagerly.

"This is one of the reasons why I hate this world," she teased. "People never learn. They'll go on holiday every year and each time, they'll declare to their new friends that they will definitely stay in touch and most certainly arrange a meetup. These people rarely stay in touch and it's even more rare they'll meet."

"So... we won't keep in touch?"

"I'm saying I have every intention to keep in touch but, if history has taught me anything... this is likely to be the last time I see or speak to you."

"Okay," I said. Some would probably have been offended by this brutal honesty. I genuinely admired it.

There were a few moments of silence before Alizia started to tease me again. "You're not going to try and kiss me again, are you?" I say she was teasing, but there were definitely fearful undertones in her voice.

I gave out a laugh and confirmed, "I'm not. No."

She proceeded to look me dead in the eyes for a good two seconds - maybe even three. It was definitely longer than what would be considered as the 'standard time' to keep someone's gaze. Surely, she wasn't about to kiss me?

Of course, she did not.

She started walking away in her typically cool and composed manner. I hoped she'd turn to look at me just one final time - anything that signalled to me that she was even the tiniest bit interested in me. This was wishful thinking and none of it would transpire.

Just as quickly as she'd entered my life, she was out of it.

Chapter Fifteen: One Month after Happys - Aiden's Story

I've lost count of the times I've almost officially requested a visit to speak to Danny Palmer at the Young Offenders Institution he'd been held at since causing the death of my father and friends.

There was a short form I needed to fill out. This was the first time I'd reached the final question but I wasn't quite ready to click the 'submit' button.

Sitting at the computer in my bedroom, I pondered on what I'd say to him face to face. It was a scenario I'd played out numerous times in my mind. I used to fantasise about being close enough to cause him severe harm, regardless of the repercussions. The scenarios I created had become less sinister as time had passed and I truly believed that I had now, finally reached a point in which I would be able to talk to him - maybe even verbally forgive him. I certainly believed I had forgiven him, but I worried that seeing him would bring the initial anger and resentment flooding back so strongly that forgiveness would be impossible.

Perhaps now was not the time to be making this monumental decision.

I was just about to shut the computer down when Tracey came storming into my room. I scrambled to open a new tab - hiding the application form like it was a shameful secret. "Knock!" I shouted to my sister.

"Sorry to interrupt your porn," she squealed, breathless. "You're not going to believe me when I tell you this."

"You just had your annual shower?" I joked.

Catching her breath, she continued, "Now... don't be angry."

I was almost certain that I was about to become pretty fucking angry.

"Go on," I said hesitantly.

"That song you sang at Happys... Don't Wake Me. I may have filmed it for my YouTube Channel and it may have just blown up. You're going viral right now!"

I took the statement with a pinch of salt. My sister once got excited about receiving ten views on one video. With that in mind, her idea of "viral" numbers probably weren't much more than... one-hundred, perhaps.

I typed the URL for Tracey's channel on my computer and to my astonishment the video - uploaded just a few hours ago - had reached more than one-hundred-thousand views. I refreshed the page a few times and with each click, the numbers continued to rise dramatically.

"How did this even happen?" I asked, utterly bewildered.

"One of my five subscribers, Alizia, happened to see the video and kind of shared it on all of her socials."

Lo and behold, right at the top of the comments section was a message from Alizia. It read, "You should totally use this footage as part of your 'My Way' funeral footage." Morbid? Perhaps. It didn't stop me grinning from ear to ear though.

Seeing this reaction, Tracey asked cautiously, "So... you're not mad?"

"A little heads up would have been nice but I'm not mad," I said softly, still rather taken by surprise. "I guess this means you can now join that content club thingy at school."

"Abi Brewer has already called to offer me a spot."

"Congratulations!"

"Thank you. I gracefully declined the offer though."

"How come?" I asked, bewildered.

"I thought it was what I wanted. I mean, it most definitely is what I wanted, but priorities change. I don't want to sell my soul for views - chasing those numbers with subject matters that may be relevant, but are not in the slightest bit interesting to me."

I was rather apprehensive as to how much truth was in her statement. "For someone that doesn't care about numbers, you seemed pretty giddy about the latest video going viral."

"Of course, it's fucking awesome!" she squealed. "However, does that mean I'm less proud of the videos that only got a dozen or less views? Not at all. Numbers are great but they don't define who I am."

Okay, she actually sounded very sincere and passionate. "I'm proud of you," I smiled.

My phone started vibrating from the top of my computer desk. I unconsciously donned another huge smile upon seeing Alizia's name flashing up on the screen. I could feel butterflies in my stomach starting to flutter.

Tracey gave me a teasing wink. "I'll leave you both to chat privately," she smirked before leaving.

I allowed my phone to ring for a few seconds so as not to appear too keen. Finally answering, I joked, "This is Aiden Gardener's assistant. Sorry, he's too busy being famous to speak to riff-raff."

"Shouldn't you be too busy ordering his latte instead of chatting to riff-raff?" she said, continuing the facade. "Seriously though, I hope you don't mind me sharing the video?"

"I've not really had a chance to process it," I explained. "But I'm trying to focus on the positives. It'll mean a lot to Tracey and, Uncle

Dave can officially say he's written a hit song. Not only that, he's now a published author."

"Really?" Alizia asked excitedly.

"...No," I laughed. "His book is truly awful. Nobody should ever have to endure the musings on those pages. Still, the song is something he can be proud of."

"Are you going to sing it at your gig tonight?"

"I guess I'll have to now that it's viral. You still able to come watch the band?"

"Of course," she replied proudly. "Your big return to the stage... I wouldn't miss it for the world."

"See you there," I said as the butterflies consumed my entire body.

"See you there."

It would be a cliché, ribbon wrapped, happy ending if I were to tell you that Alizia and I were now a couple. We were not and I couldn't have been more content with that - and no, I'm not forcing those words out through gritted teeth.

There's countless movies out there that will have you convinced that if the guy doesn't end up in a relationship with the girl, he ain't shit. Label or no label... Alizia and I had just supported each other through some really difficult weeks with no sign of this bond ending at any point soon.

The most amazing girl I'd ever met was my friend. That was enough - more than enough. I was the luckiest guy in the world.

Just as I was about to close the YouTube tab on my computer, a recommended video caught my eye. The image showed Lee Lauren looking tearful and although my gut feeling screamed that this was nothing more than clickbait, I was curious enough to investigate further.

The video was titled, 'Discussing the Jenny Happy Rumours'. This surely couldn't have been in reference to the same Jenny that was related to the owner of Happys Holidays? I was now even more intrigued.

Right off the bat, the idiot was giving an Oscar-worthy performance with the waterworks set to maximum. "Firstly, I'd like to thank my true fans for believing me," he cried. This came across as rather manipulative. I had no idea what this was in reference to, but to imply people couldn't have been 'true fans' if they casted doubt on anything he had to say… well, that was a classic dick move from him.

Lee continued, "I've heard the lies and rumours. Let me make this completely clear again… I did not make unwanted - or any kind of sexual advances towards this Jenny Happy girl. Her video is full of lies. Yes, I met her last year whilst on holiday but did nothing more than gracefully accept her request for photos. There are also rumours that I had accepted the offer to make this Happys advert through guilt or some kind of leverage from her father. Again, not true. I did the advert solely for the money. A lot of money. I am already in touch with my lawyer to discuss this defamation of character."

I looked at the upload date of the video. It had only been posted about an hour ago - which made sense as I'm almost certain this would have been brought to my attention by now, had it been any sooner.

Another one of Lee's videos was listed under the recommendation section. Surprisingly, it was even more recent than the last - having been uploaded just ten minutes ago. It was simply titled, "Sos."

As much as it pained me to endure more of his content, I found myself falling down the rabbit hole. I was invested.

An observation upon clicking this video was that the teen idol no longer seemed upset, but rather stand-offish. "I've seen the hidden camera footage posted by Jenny Happy," he said. "I am already in touch with my lawyer to discuss this clear entrapment - not to mention the laws against filming someone without their consent. I would like to stress that not once did Jenny mention her age to me when we met. Nor was there any actual physical penetration. I can, however, see why some would say I came on strong asking for it. Moving forward, I shall also be seeking help for my disease and would like to thank the true fans for recognising how hard it is being a sex addict. No pun intended. Finally, for anyone I have upset or offended... sincerely... sos."

I thought back to when I first met Lee, after he'd intentionally smacked the back of my head at the Happys welcome event. What I received after that physical contact was the worst apology I'd ever heard... until now. If he really was in touch with his solicitors, I'm pretty sure they'd be begging him for all future "apologies" to be worded by them.

As much as I wanted to see how this story progressed, I had a gig to get ready for. As the only member of my band that wouldn't be drinking alcohol, I was the designated driver and therefore had to pick up each member. There were also the instruments that needed loading into the van and the invoice to print out. Lots to do - but not before taking one last look at the Young Offenders Institution visitor application form on the monitor. "Fuck it," I said before finally clicking the submit button.

This visit was to be the final major hurdle before the grieving process could officially commence. With Alizia by my side, I knew I could do it. I could do anything.

Here's one of the reasons why I love this world. Every now and then - often when you least expect it - people come into your life and make it so much better. During the weekend at Happys and beyond, Alizia helped me to see the world a little bit brighter. Actually, a lot brighter. As our friendship grew, so did her positive influence on me. She pushed me further than I ever thought was possible and as a result, I achieved greater things. I could now see the positives in my life that had not long ago been hiding in plain sight. I once again felt like the person I was before Dad had died and I no longer felt hate towards this world or the people in it. It was now so much easier to see the best in people. Not Lee, obviously. He can fuck off.

The end.

Acknowledgments

After two decades of waking up every New Year's Day, saying "This is the year I finally write a book," I've only gone and done it – hurrah! This wouldn't have been possible without the help and support of many people I'm privileged to have in my life. Whether it be proof-reading, helping with the cover, inspiring characters, motivating me to finally take action or encouraging my creative journey – sincerely, thank you to each and every one of you.

Mum, Ken, Marian, Sarah, Erin, Neil, Johnny, Roe, Karina, Ross, Nats, Heidi, Sharon, Trystan, Wendy, Stu, Lindsey, Laura-Jayne, Sean, Bethany, Gav, Farrell, Rachel, Wayne, Marc, Alex, Helena, Emma, Pep, Becky, Ian & Rachael – in one way or another you've supported or inspired me. Again, thank you.

Also, a huge thanks to anyone reading this. There's a lot of competition out there with so many other books you could have chosen – yet here you are, reading mine. That means more to me than you know.

Finally, I'd like to dedicate this book to three people in particular…

My son. Aiden, you inspire me to be a better person and I'm constantly working on myself to be the best dad I can possibly be. You are my absolute world and I love you so much. I hope this novel makes you proud and encourages you to follow your dreams too. If someone as easily distracted as me can finish writing a book, you can achieve anything.

Nan was my childhood hero and I loved visiting her home. Towards the end of her life, Alzheimer's sadly changed her personality beyond recognition. Because of this, some people were never given the pleasure of meeting the colourful character I grew up with. Should this horrible disease one day consume me too, I want people to know that my brain was once capable of great things (alright Clarkey, we'd all like to be our own critic).

Finally, Mum, thank you for being such a positive role-model in my life. Not everyone I grew up with was the kindest of people (putting it nicely) but I always had your wonderful self to teach me right from wrong. I make mistakes, of course, but I at least strive to do good and that is thanks to you.

Printed in Great Britain
by Amazon

85609266R00098